A HANDBOOK
FOR EXPERT WITNESSES
IN CHILDREN ACT CASES

Two week
loan

Please return on or before the last
date stamped below.
Charges are made for late return.

A HANDBOOK
FOR EXPERT WITNESSES
IN CHILDREN ACT CASES

NICHOLAS WALL
*A Judge of the High Court and
Family Division Liaison Judge for the
Northern Circuit*

Family Law

2000

Published by
Family Law
a publishing imprint of
Jordan Publishing Limited
21 St Thomas Street
Bristol BS1 6JS

British Library Cataloguing-in-Publication Data

A catalogue record for this book is available
from the British Library.

ISBN 0 85308 628 1

Photoset by Mendip Communications Ltd, Frome, Somerset
Printed in Great Britain by MPG Books, Bodmin, Cornwall

Foreword

The contribution of the medical expert witness is a crucial part of the decision-making process in many difficult child cases which come before the family courts. The courts are increasingly relying upon the medical evidence, mainly in cases of physical, emotional and sexual abuse.

Delay in family cases, particularly child cases, is a serious problem. It is very important that those who give evidence assist in getting the case to court within a reasonable time and are able to provide the court with the most useful information in the most succinct and digestible form so as to minimise both the time spent in court and the inconvenience to the witness who has other equally important duties to perform elsewhere. The clear presentation of the report, the pre-court discussions and exchange of views between experts, the concentration upon the issues genuinely in dispute, all help towards the efficient and expeditious disposal of child cases.

The reliance of the court upon the medical expert places a considerable burden upon him/her to provide an impartial and objective assessment of the situation with recommendations based upon the welfare of the child concerned.

This handbook, written by a family judge with enormous experience of medical evidence, is down to earth, practical and witness-friendly. The author understands the medical perspective and provides the expert, who is faced with a request to provide a report and give evidence in court, with a simple and step-by-step set of guidelines to show what are his/her duties and how to approach each part of the case. It deals, for instance, with joint instructions, writing the report, giving evidence and limits upon the advice to give to the judge. It is a most valuable source of general information for medical experts in family cases and also for lawyers and all those who instruct the medical profession as well as those who try the cases. I hope it may also have the effect of encouraging more health professionals to become expert witnesses. I commend this book to all those involved in difficult child cases which require the calling of medical evidence.

ELIZABETH BUTLER-SLOSS

Introduction

This handbook has three principal purposes. The first is to provide practical advice and guidance for expert witnesses instructed to prepare reports and give evidence in proceedings under the Children Act 1989 in England and Wales. The second is to encourage doctors and mental health professionals who have expertise in relation to children to undertake work in Children Act proceedings as expert witnesses. The third is to raise standards and harmonise good practice both amongst the judiciary making orders for expert evidence under the Children Act 1989, and amongst practitioners who seek such orders and then have to put them into effect.

Since the implementation of the Children Act 1989 in October 1991, there has undoubtedly been a growing reliance by the courts on expert evidence in the context of the physical and sexual abuse of children, as well as in cases of physical and emotional neglect and in relation to the assessment of children's relationships with their parents and the risks posed to children by any given placement. At the same time, the pool of experts willing and able to undertake the work is small and, in some parts of the country, for example on the Northern Circuit, demand substantially exceeds supply.

In the years since the implementation of the Children Act, there has also been a growth of case-law decided mostly by the Court of Appeal and the judges of the Family Division relating both to the jurisprudential basis upon which the courts approach expert evidence in proceedings relating to children, as well as practical issues such as time-tabling and report writing.

This handbook will seek to explain the way in which the courts hearing proceedings relating to children approach expert evidence. It aims to dispel misunderstandings and to help medical and mental health professionals to an awareness and understanding of the important legal developments which have been taking place. By these means, the book aims to encourage more suitably qualified experts to take on this very important work.

As a general rule, doctors do not read the law reports, and lawyers do not read medical journals. Thus, despite much excellent inter-disciplinary work and a number of good articles both in the legal and the medical press, there appears to be a continuing level of misunderstanding between the medical and legal professions about what is expected by the courts of expert witnesses in proceedings under the Children Act.

In particular, some experts seem unsure about what they can and cannot do both when preparing expert opinions for court and when appearing in court. Equally, the legal profession continues from time to time to treat expert witnesses in a cavalier fashion, seeming to think that they can be called to court at will, and showing no understanding of their clinical responsibilities.

Expert witnesses are crucial to the proper operation of family proceedings. Courts are often dependent for their decisions on the quality of the medical evidence they receive and the integrity of those who give it. Through multi-disciplinary co-operation, judges and advocates increasingly understand that preparing a report and coming to court to give evidence are time-consuming and take doctors away from their clinical responsibilities. Efforts have been made by the judges to address these issues.

On the other side of the equation, many doctors still see the courtroom in family proceedings as a hostile environment, and some perceive the purpose of cross-examination as being to impugn their professional integrity by means of a personal attack on their credibility.

If this book can help to dispel myths and to help establish good practice, it will have achieved its objective. It encourages experts to be more proactive in their approach to report writing and not to feel that they are at the mercy of the judiciary and the legal profession.

Proceedings relating to children are in a special category of litigation. In the vast majority of cases, the welfare of the child is the court's paramount consideration. Expert witnesses must adopt the same approach. As the opening chapters of this book make clear, the expert instructed in Children Act proceedings writes an opinion for the *court* to assist the *court* in fulfilling its duty to the child. Thus, neither the partisan expert, nor the expert who has a particular hobby-horse to ride, is wanted in family proceedings.

Expert witnesses need to remember that most judges do not have any more medical expertise than the average intelligent lay person. It is for this reason that they rely heavily on expert opinion, and are dependent upon the integrity of expert witnesses.

It is to be hoped that this book, which, for a trial period, will be supplied with the letter of instruction to all experts instructed to advise the courts in family proceedings on the Northern Circuit, will assist and reassure doctors about the importance of their role, and give them practical guidance about what they can and cannot properly do.

I am very conscious, from feedback which I have received that, in practice, many of the guidelines for good practice for lawyers which I have described in this book are not being followed on the ground. Aspirations are of no use if they are not implemented. This book will thus also be circulated to all the judiciary on circuit who hear family cases, and attempts will be made to ensure that it is read by lawyers practising in the field.

The text is addressed directly to experts in the second person plural in the hope that this will make it more immediately and apparently relevant. The chapter on fees has been contributed by Iain Hamilton, solicitor and Recorder.

I have, wherever possible, avoided direct references to decided cases in the text. A suggested reading list for further reference is given in Appendix 1.

A number of professional witnesses who read this book in manuscript suggested that it would be helpful to have a chapter giving some answers to specific questions which they had encountered in practice. In the event, space does not permit me to do this: in addition, I suspect that such a chapter would be like the 'Help' facility on most computer programs, which, frustratingly, never seems to address the particular problem with which you are wrestling. I have, therefore, attempted to deal with most of the issues which were suggested to me in the body of the text.

However, if this book does not answer practical questions or give experts the help they need, I hope that they will tell me so. Guidance such as I have offered in this book is not intended to be written in stone, and will benefit from being modified and updated. Comments and feedback from expert witnesses, the judiciary and practitioners will therefore be welcomed. Any correspondence should be addressed to me c/o the Circuit Administrator, Northern Circuit, 15 Quay Street, Manchester M60 9FD.

NICHOLAS WALL
March 2000

Acknowledgements

I owe many debts to many people for their help in the preparation of this handbook. My first thanks must be to Professor Sir Roy Meadow, who suggested the idea to me in the first place, kindly read the manuscript and made a number of helpful suggestions.

Amongst others who read the manuscript and provided trenchant, detailed and invaluable comments were Dr Frank Bamford, Professor Helen Carty, Professor Tim David and Dr Carole Kaplan.

Many judges and practitioners on the Northern Circuit have also given me hope and encouragement, notably the Designated Family Judge for Blackburn, His Honour Judge David Gee; the Designated Family Judge for Greater Manchester, His Honour Judge Allweis; and His Honour Judge Charles Bloom QC. Amongst practitioners, I am particularly grateful to Kathyrn Hughes, Recorder and Partner in Farleys, solicitors, who, with David Harris QC, Maureen Roddy of counsel and others, is part of an imaginative Northern Circuit initiative to encourage and train doctors to become expert witnesses in family proceedings. The same initiative aims to provide a register of expert witnesses available to take on cases relating to children in the North West. This handbook should be seen as my contribution to that initiative.

Iain Hamilton has not only contributed a chapter on costs: his suggestions for, and comments on, other chapters warrant joint authorship of the whole.

Any errors are, of course, my responsibility.

It has been a great privilege for me to have been the Family Division Liaison Judge for the Northern Circuit over the past four years. I have come to have a profound respect for the quality and dedication of practitioners from all the disciplines working in the Family Justice System in the North West. Typically, all those who have assisted in the preparation of this handbook live busy professional lives, yet have given freely of their time and expertise.

If the slimness of the volume can bear the weight, I would like to dedicate this handbook to all my friends and colleagues from every discipline working within the Family Justice System on the Northern Circuit.

Finally, I would like to thank the President for her support, and for writing the Foreword.

NICHOLAS WALL
March 2000

Contents

Appendices

Chapter One

Why Am I Doing This?

1.1   You find yourself instructed to write a report and appear in court in family proceedings under the Children Act 1989. This may be because you were the treating paediatrician in a suspected case of non-accidental injury, or because a second opinion is required on the treating doctor's diagnosis. It may be that you are a radiologist whose opinion is sought on the significance of X-rays or brain scans. It may be that you are a psychiatrist whose opinion is sought on whether or not a child has been sexually abused. You may be a psychologist instructed to make an assessment of a parent's capacity to care for children in a case of chronic emotional or physical neglect. There may be a number of other reasons for your involvement in the case.

1.2   Writing a court report in proceedings under the Children Act 1989 and appearing in court in care proceedings may be a new experience for you. It may be unfamiliar territory. Finding the time to read the documents in the case, interviewing the parties and/or the child, writing your report and organising your diary to enable you to give evidence in court may all appear excessively time-consuming. Why are you doing it?

1.3   From the court's perspective, you are doing it because the court has asked you to. A principal theme of this book is that, although your formal instructions come from the solicitors for one or more of the parties, you are being asked for your opinion because the court wants it, and because the court has given permission for you to see the court papers.

1.4   Expert evidence is often of critical importance in a difficult child case. Sometimes it is determinative of a child's future. The court therefore places substantial reliance on the professional integrity of the experts who advise it. The point to bear in mind throughout is that you are involved in the case to assist the judge reach the right result for the child or children in the case. I make no apology for repeating this particular message at different points in this book.

1.5   Judges and lawyers increasingly recognise the demands which they make on expert witnesses. Good practice now requires that great care should be taken over the instruction of expert witnesses and the briefs you are given.[1] Efforts should also be made to ensure that you have sufficient time in which to prepare your opinions and that your court appearances are time-tabled to fit in with your other professional commitments.

1.6 This book is concerned with what should be happening. It is one thing for judges to say what good practice should be – another to put it into effect. So you may still find that the lawyers who commissioned your report and fixed a date for you to give evidence fail to tell you that the case has been adjourned or that your evidence is no longer required, with the result that you turn up at court only to be sent away again – or get a message on your mobile telephone as you are driving to court. You may still find t' t when you get to court you are kept hanging about, or asked to com ack on another day. These are examples of bad practice which th k hopes to reduce and, in an ideal world, eliminate.

1.7 T book therefore aims to set out not only what is expected of expert witnesses in proceedings under the Children Act, but also what expert witness an reasonably expect from the court and from the lawyers involved in the case.

1.8 If your experience is that the good practice set out in this book is not being followed, it is important that you make your views known. If you have a bad experience, you should complain. Chapter 22 tells you how to do so.

Note

1   See, for example, *Re G (Minors) (Expert Witnesses)* [1994] 2 FLR 291, an extract from which is set out at Appendix 3.

Chapter Two

The Approach of the Court to Expert Evidence in Family Proceedings: Three Cardinal Principles

2.1   Three cardinal principles underlie the approach of the court to expert evidence in family proceedings, and it is very important that you should understand all three, as they govern the approach which the court will expect you to adopt in writing your report and in giving evidence. The three principles are:

(1) *The proceedings are non-adversarial*. This means that the court is not concerned with whether one side or the other will succeed in achieving the result which that side wants. The court is concerned with the welfare of the children who are the subject of the proceedings: their welfare is the court's paramount consideration and the views and aspirations of the other parties to the proceedings are relevant only insofar as they reflect on the welfare of the children involved.

(2) *The proceedings are confidential*. Statements and other papers generated by the court process in family proceedings are confidential to the court, and it is a contempt of court to disclose them to a person who is not a party to the proceedings without the court's permission. It follows that an expert can be instructed and shown the court papers only with the permission of the judge who, in turn, decides both what issues require expert evidence and the brief the expert should be given.

Furthermore, the Family Proceedings Rules 1991 provide, by rule 4.18(1), that 'no person may, without the leave of the court, cause the child to be medically or psychiatrically examined, or otherwise assessed, for the purpose of the preparation of expert evidence for use in the proceedings'.

(3) *Litigation privilege does not apply*. This means that a party who has commissioned a report from an expert witness cannot refuse to disclose the report to the judge and to the other parties to the proceedings. Whatever the report contains, and whether or not it supports the case being put forward by the party who commissioned it, it must be disclosed.

What these principles mean for the expert witness

2.2   These three principles are all fundamental to the way in which you should approach your task if you are instructed in family proceedings.

Non-adversarial

2.3   The phrase 'non-adversarial' should not be misunderstood. Of course there will be issues of fact in family proceedings which the court will have to decide on the balance of probabilities in the normal way. Most expert evidence goes to factual issues. Obvious examples are: has this child been sexually abused? Was this a non-accidental injury? If it was, what was the likely timing and mechanism of the injury?

2.4   Medical evidence which goes to issues such as these will be tested in the normal way by cross-examination, and the judge will have to decide, on the balance of probabilities, what happened. The importance of the non-adversarial principle for you is that you are not there to support one side or the other. You are there to give your objective professional opinion to the judge on the points which are within the area of your expertise in order to assist the judge to reach a conclusion which is in the best interests of the child or children concerned.

2.5   Family proceedings thus have a quasi investigative/ administrative quality in which the court seeks the outcome which will best promote, or be least detrimental to, the welfare of the child. For this reason, the strict rules of evidence are relaxed, and hearsay evidence is admissible.

2.6   For these reasons, you owe your duty to the court and to the children involved in the case, not to the party who commissioned the report from you. You report to the judge, and when you are called to give evidence, you give your evidence to the judge.

Confidentiality

The confidentiality of the proceedings

2.7   This phrase also should not be misunderstood. What it means is that the information contained in the papers filed with the court for the purposes of the proceedings is confidential to the court. Thus, the court papers can be disclosed to people who are not parties to the proceedings only with the court's permission; and publication outside the proceedings of information relating to the proceedings is a contempt of court unless permission for it has been given by the court.

2.8   The fact that the court papers are confidential does not, however, prevent you from discussing the case with other experts or professionals engaged in the case. This topic is covered in more detail in Chapter 10.

2.9   Confidentiality, as discussed in this chapter, is not to be confused with the confidential relationship between patient and doctor. It does not mean that, in the course of your enquiries, parties to the proceedings or any witnesses whom you interview can tell you anything 'in confidence' which cannot then be revealed to the court. Rather to the contrary, as described in more detail in Chapter 13, there is no such thing as an 'off the record' discussion for an expert instructed in proceedings relating to children. Any piece of information which you obtain during the course of your enquiries which is relevant to your report must be disclosed in it.

2.10   It has to be recognised in the context of proceedings relating to children that, for example, the inability of a parent to provide information 'in confidence' to an expert may cause difficulties both for the parent and the expert. Parents, when you interview them, may wish to behave as they would in a medical consultation and give you confidential information which they might not provide in other circumstances. They may also be inhibited in telling you the truth for fear of a criminal prosecution if incriminating admissions are made.

2.11   For your purposes, however, the rule is clear. You are making enquiries within the proceedings for the purpose of making a report to the court. If, in these circumstances, you obtain information which is relevant to the welfare of the children with whom the court is concerned, it must be shared with the other parties and given to the court. It will then be for the court to decide if it should be passed on to any third party such as the police.[1]

Disclosure

2.12   Your report will be disclosed to the judge, to the other parties to the proceedings, and to any other experts instructed in the case, irrespective of whether or not it supports the case of the party who commissioned it.

2.13   Disclosure has two particular implications for you.

(1) The court will expect your report to be objective and wholly free from bias. You must avoid any attempt to write a report which is inappropriately slanted towards the commissioning party. Such an approach will be deprecated by the court and will devalue your evidence.

(2) Because the report will be read not only by the judge but by the other parties and any other experts instructed in the case, your professional integrity is at stake with every report you write.

Summary

2.14   If you are instructed to write a report in family proceedings, your duty is to the court and to the child, not to the party who commissions the report. You cannot receive information 'in confidence' from anybody. All relevant information must be shared with the other parties and the court. Your report will be disclosed whatever it says. Your duty is to be objective and wholly free from any bias in favour of one party or the other.

Note

1   Section 98 of the Children Act 1989 does give parents some protection against self-incrimination. It provides that, in proceedings under the Act, no one can be excused from giving evidence, or answering any question whilst giving evidence, on the ground that the answer may incriminate them or their spouse, but that any such statement or admission made in the proceedings is not admissible in evidence in any other criminal proceedings against them or their spouse apart from perjury. However, where a father made an admission in care proceedings that he had caused injuries to a child leading to that child's death, the Court of Appeal ordered disclosure to the police of a transcript of his evidence on the basis that the public interest in the administration of justice overrode the public interest in confidentiality and frankness in proceedings relating to children: see *In Re C (A Minor) (Care Proceedings: Disclosure)* [1997] Fam 76. Note also that a social worker engaged in an inter-agency investigation into child abuse does not need to seek the leave of the court before informing the police about any statement or admission made by a parent.

Chapter Three

The Respective Roles of Expert and Judge: Why the Professional Integrity of Experts is so Important

3.1 It will help you when writing a report and giving evidence in family proceedings if you bear in mind throughout the respective functions of expert and judge.

3.2 You form an assessment and express your opinion within the particular area of your expertise. Judges decide particular issues in individual cases on all the evidence available to the court.

3.3 Your function is to advise the judge. You do not decide the case or any issue in the case.

3.4 The corollary to this is that it is not for the judge to become involved in medical controversy except in the extremely rare case where such a controversy is itself an issue in the case, and a judicial assessment of it becomes necessary for the proper resolution of the proceedings.

3.5 The reason for this is obvious. Whilst judges have knowledge and experience from practice and previous cases, they rarely have more medical knowledge than the intelligent lay person: judges, almost by definition, are not experts in the field about which you are giving evidence.

3.6 Judges bring to the inquiry forensic and analytical skills, and have the unique advantage over the parties and the witnesses in the case that they alone are in a position to weigh all its multifarious facets. This process, of course, involves an evaluation of your opinion in the context of the court's duty to make findings of fact and assessments of the credibility of witnesses.

3.7 It follows that the dependence of the court on the skill, knowledge and, above all, the professional and intellectual integrity of the expert witness cannot be over-emphasised. Judges have a difficult enough task as it is in sensitive child cases. To have, in addition, to resolve a subtle and complex medical disagreement or to make assessments of the reliability of expert witnesses not only adds immeasurably to the judges' task, but given their fallibility and lack of medical training, may help to lead them to false conclusions.

3.8   It is partly for this reason that the current practice of the courts in children cases is to require disclosure of all medical reports (see **2.8** et seq) and to invite the experts to confer pre-trial (see Chapters 10 and 11).

The standard of proof

3.9   Although it is for judges to decide what happened in cases where the facts are in dispute, your opinion will often be a crucial element in helping the judge form a view. The obvious example is an injury which a parent claims has an innocent cause. It is for the judge to decide:

(1) how the injury occurred; and
(2) who was responsible for it.

Your role is nearly always limited to helping the judge on (1).

3.10   Judges decide disputed issues of fact in proceedings under the Children Act on the civil standard of proof known as 'the balance of probability'. This is a lower standard than that used in criminal proceedings to decide guilt, which is 'beyond reasonable doubt'.

3.11   The balance of probability test means simply that a court can be satisfied that an event occurred if it considers that, on the evidence before the court, the occurrence of the event was more likely than not.

3.12   However, in *Re H (Minors) (Sexual Abuse: Standard of Proof)*,[1] a decision of the House of Lords, the majority opinion was that certainty was seldom attainable, and probability was an unsatisfactorily vague criterion because there were degrees of probability. Lord Nicholls of Birkenhead, giving the majority opinion, therefore added a rider to the 'balance of probability test' to the effect that the more serious or improbable the allegation of abuse, the more convincing was the evidence required to prove the allegation.[2]

3.13   This decision has relevance for you only insofar as you may be asked, for example, to express an opinion on the degree of likelihood or probability of an injury having been caused in a particular way, or whether a child has been sexually abused. You should not be troubled by this. The process of differential diagnosis requires the systematic evaluation of the clinical evidence, and diagnoses of different conditions are reached with differing degrees of confidence.

3.14   In the context of a finding of fact to be made by a judge, the safest way of expressing your opinion about a particular injury or condition is that it is 'consistent' or 'inconsistent' with a given set of facts. Plainly, however, degrees of likelihood are also involved in this analysis. Some clinical signs are pathognomonic of abuse. In such a case, you are entitled to say that the condition is consistent only with abuse.

3.15   The *Re H* test is, of course, for lawyers, not for doctors. If you find its analysis helpful in forming a diagnosis, you should feel free to adopt it. Essentially, however, what the judge is looking for is your clinical assessment and a diagnosis based on clinical expertise.

Summary

3.16   Judges decide cases; experts advise them on points specifically within the area of the expert's expertise. Judges rely heavily on the integrity of experts, and encourage experts to agree whenever that is possible. Judges are not equipped to engage in medical controversy. Judges decide disputed factual issues on the balance of probability. The function of the expert is to advise the judge whether the injuries are consistent with particular facts.

Notes

1   [1996] AC 563.
2   The relevant passage in the speech of Lord Nicholls reads as follows:

> 'The balance of probability standard means that a court is satisfied an event occurred if the court considers that, on the evidence, the occurrence of the event was more likely than not. When assessing the probabilities the court will have in mind as a factor, to whatever extent is appropriate in the particular case, that the more serious the allegation the less likely it is that the event occurred and, hence, the stronger should be the evidence before the court concludes that the allegation is established on the balance of probability. Fraud is usually less likely than negligence. Deliberate physical injury is usually less likely than accidental physical injury. A stepfather is usually less likely to have repeatedly raped and had non-consensual oral sex with his under age stepdaughter than on some occasion to have lost his temper and slapped her. Built into the preponderance of probability standard is a generous degree of flexibility in respect of the seriousness of the allegation.'

Chapter Four

The General Duties of Experts

4.1 The general duties which you owe when writing opinions for use in court and when giving evidence are very clear and apply in every type of proceedings. They were well expressed by Mr Justice Cresswell sitting in the Commercial Court in 1993 in a case known as *The Ikarian Reefer.*[1]

4.2 Mr Justice Cresswell said that the duties and responsibilities of expert witnesses included the following:

(1) Expert evidence presented to the Court should be and seen to be the independent product of the expert uninfluenced as to form or content by the exigencies of litigation.

(2) An expert witness should provide independent assistance to the court by way of objective unbiased opinion in relation to matters within his expertise. An expert witness in the High Court should never assume the role of advocate.

(3) An expert witness should state the facts or assumptions on which his opinion is based. He should not omit to consider material facts which detract from his concluded opinion.

(4) An expert witness should make it clear when a particular question or issue falls outside his expertise.

(5) If an expert's opinion is not properly researched because he considers that insufficient data is available then this must be stated with an indication that the opinion is no more than a provisional one.

(6) If after exchange of reports, an expert witness changes his view on a material matter, such change of view should be communicated to the other side without delay and when appropriate to the Court.

(7) Where expert evidence refers to photographs, plans, calculations survey reports or other similar documents these must be provided to the opposite party at the same time as the exchange of reports.

Particular duties in family proceedings

4.3   In relation specifically to family proceedings, the most
important statement of principle is to be found in *Re R*,[2] a decision of
Mr Justice Cazalet in 1991, in which he said:

(1) Expert witnesses are in a privileged position; indeed, only experts
     are permitted to give an *opinion* in evidence. Outside the legal field
     the court itself has no expertise and for that reason frequently has
     to rely on the evidence of experts.

(2) Such experts must express only opinions which they genuinely hold
     and which are not biased in favour of one particular party.
     Opinions can, of course, differ and indeed quite frequently experts
     who have expressed their objective and honest opinion will differ,
     but such differences are usually within a legitimate area of
     disagreement.

(3) Experts should not mislead by omissions. They should consider all
     the material facts in reaching their conclusions and must not omit
     to consider the material facts which could detract from their
     concluded opinion.

(4) If experts look for and report on factors which tend to support a
     particular proposition or case, their report should still;

     (a) provide a straightforward, not a misleading opinion;
     (b) be objective and not omit factors which do not support their
          opinion; and
     (c) be properly researched.

(5) If the expert's opinion is not properly researched because he or she
     considers that insufficient data is available, then the expert must say
     so and indicate that the opinion is no more than a provisional one.

(6) In certain circumstances experts may find that they have to give
     opinions adverse to the party which instructed them. Alternatively
     if, contrary to the appropriate practice and expert does provide a
     report which is other than wholly objective – that is one which
     seeks to 'promote' a particular case – the report must make this
     clear. However, such an approach should be avoided because it
     would (a) be an abuse of the position of the expert's proper
     function and privilege and (b) render the report an argument, not an
     opinion.

The dangers arising from a misleading or tendentious opinion: the duty not to mislead

4.4   You should always bear in mind that a misleading opinion may inhibit a proper assessment of a particular case by the non-medical professional advisers and may also lead parties, and in particular parents, to false views and hopes.

4.5   Furthermore, such misleading expert opinions are likely to increase costs by requiring competing evidence to be called at the hearing on issues which should in fact be non-contentious.

4.6   In children cases, your duty to be objective and not to mislead is especially vital because the child's welfare, which is paramount, is at stake. An absence of objectivity may result in a child being wrongly placed and thereby unnecessarily at risk.

Summary

4.7   What the court expects from you is an objective, independent, well-researched, thorough opinion, which takes account of all relevant information and which represents your genuine professional view on the issues submitted to you.

Notes

1   More fully, *National Justice Compania Naviera SA v Prudential Assurance Co Ltd* [1993] 2 Lloyd's Rep 68.
2   *Note: Re R (A Minor) (Experts' Evidence)* [1991] 1 FLR 291.

Chapter Five

What you can Advise the Judge about

5.1 As stated in Chapter 4, your function is to give your advice to the court on any issue properly within the area of your expertise. You do not decide the case: that is the function of the judge.

5.2 By virtue of section 3(1) of the Civil Evidence Act 1972, your opinion on any relevant matter on which you are qualified to give expert evidence is admissible in evidence.

5.3 Accordingly, whilst it is for the judge to decide, for example, whether a child has been sexually abused, or is to be believed when recounting allegations of sexual abuse, you are entitled, if you have the relevant expertise, to tell the judge that in your opinion the child has been sexually abused or that the child is credible when he or she relates allegations of abuse.

5.4 You should, however, be very cautious when advising a judge that in your opinion a particular event occurred. You should do this only if you feel you have all the relevant information and that the expression of such an opinion is both truly within the area of your expertise and a necessary part of your decision-making process. The judge will have to decide the question on all the evidence in the case, including the oral evidence given in the witness-box. You will not have access to all that information, and the expression of a categorical opinion which may be invalidated by material not within your knowledge will – at the very least – substantially devalue your evidence.

Summary

5.5 You are free to express an opinion about any issue in the case, including those which it is the province of the judge to decide, provided your expression of opinion relates to a matter on which you are qualified to give expert evidence. You should, however, be cautious about expressing firm opinions on events which may or may not have occurred and about which you may not have all the relevant information.

Chapter Six

Preliminary Enquiries of the Expert

6.1   The first enquiry about the feasibility of you giving an opinion in a case will usually come from a solicitor acting for one of the parties, including of course the solicitor who is acting for the child. It will often take the form of a telephone call enquiring about your availability to do the work within a given time-frame and giving only a broad outline of what is required.

6.2   Before you accept instructions to act in a case you should know:

(a) the nature of the proceedings and the issues to be decided by the court;

(b) the precise nature of the issue or issues which you are to be asked to address;

(c) whether or not leave has already been given for the papers to be disclosed to you or to another expert in your field;

(d) the volume of reading which you will be required to undertake;

(e) whether or not (in an appropriate case) permission has been given for you to examine the child; and whether or not it will be necessary for you to conduct interviews (and if so with whom);

(f) the time-scale within which your opinion is required;

(g) whether a date has been fixed for the hearing and whether or not you are likely to be required to give evidence.

6.3   It is of the greatest importance for the proper planning and time-tabling of a case in which you are approached to give your opinion, that you should be given adequate information before agreeing to do so.

6.4   You should, in return, make clear:

(a) that the work required is within the area of your expertise;

(b) your ability to do the relevant work within a specified time scale;

(c) your availability to give evidence, in particular dates and times to avoid, and, where a hearing date has not been fixed, the amount of notice you will require to enable you conveniently to arrange a time to come to court without undue disruption to your normal clinical work.

Summary

6.5 Where your opinion is sought in a child case, you should agree to give it only if the question on which you are asked to advise is within the area of your expertise and if you are able to comply with the conditions laid down by the court for the making of your enquiries, and delivery of your report.

Chapter Seven

The Nature of the Brief Given by the Court

7.1   It is very important for you to appreciate that your brief comes from the court. You must, accordingly, work to that brief. Good practice requires that the issues on which expert evidence may be required should be identified by the parties and the court at the earliest possible opportunity. Thus, the need to instruct experts; the issues which they are required to address; and the nature of the different disciplines required to address the relevant issues are all debated before the court at an early directions appointment.[1]

7.2   It is, however, also very important that you should feel comfortable with the brief which you are given. There is a misconception amongst some experts that the brief is written in stone and you cannot deviate from it. This is not the case. If you cannot work to the brief given to you by the court, you should immediately say so, and either refuse to act or invite the solicitor who has commissioned the report to return to the court to seek a variation in the brief. The court will pay considerable regard to a carefully expressed statement of your areas of expertise, your professional standards and your methods of work.

7.3   For example, in most cases where either a physical examination or a psychiatric or psychological assessment of a child is required, the court will normally allow the child to be examined or interviewed by only one expert. This is often an expert instructed by the child's guardian ad litem, or by the guardian ad litem and the other parties jointly. If one of the parties subsequently seeks a second opinion from you, and if the court gives permission for a second opinion but refuses permission for you to see the child, you should only accept the brief if you feel that you can properly do the work without seeing the child.

7.4   In other cases, the court may seek advice on how a particular course of action can be put into effect, for example restarting contact between a child and an estranged parent. If the brief prohibits you from considering the merits of restarting contact and if you feel that you cannot properly advise without considering that question, you should, once again, either refuse the brief or seek to have it modified.

Summary

7.5   Generally speaking, you should be proactive in ensuring:

(a) that the brief you are given is appropriate;
(b) that the questions on which you are asked to advise are fairly and squarely within your expertise; and
(c) that you are given access to all the relevant people and material necessary for the formation of your opinion.

Note

1   See the extract from *Re G (Minors) (Expert Witnesses)* [1994] 2 FLR 291 set out in Appendix 3.

8.1   Your letter of instruction is a very important document. It is the practice of courts hearing family proceedings to require the letter of instruction to you to be made available to the court and to the other parties. This is part and parcel of the policy of openness which operates in family proceedings, and should ensure that you are appropriately instructed.

8.2   Sometimes you will be instructed jointly by the parties and the letter of instruction to you is agreed between their respective solicitors. This situation is covered in greater detail in Chapter 13.

8.3   Where you are instructed by one party only, the other parties will see the letter of instruction and each may, with the agreement of the other parties or the permission of the court, provide additional information or points for you to consider. None of this, of course, affects your duty to give an unbiased opinion as set out in Chapter 4.

8.4   It is essential, if you are asked to give an opinion in a child case, that you are fully instructed in relation to the area of the case on which your advice is sought. The letter of instruction should therefore always set out the context in which your opinion is sought and define carefully the specific questions you are being asked to address. If it does not do so, you should immediately seek clarification from the solicitor(s) who commissioned the report.

8.5   It is also critically important that you only give opinions which are within the ambit of your expertise. Not only, therefore, should the letter of instruction carefully define the questions which you are being asked to address; you also have an obligation to ensure that you are happy with the ambit of the task allotted to you in the proceedings. If you feel that it is either too narrow or too wide, you should not hesitate to say so.

8.6   Careful thought should have been given to the selection of the papers to be sent to you with the letter of instruction. The letter of instruction should always list the documents which are sent. The best solicitors will send you an indexed and paginated bundle of documents which, ideally, will be the same as the bundle being used by the court. You can then cross-reference to this bundle in your report.

8.7   You will not want to spend valuable time reading through papers which are irrelevant to the opinion which you are being asked to give. On the other hand, if you venture an opinion on inadequate material, there is a substantial risk that your opinion may be unsound.

8.8   You should therefore not hesitate to request further information and ask for additional documentation if you think this necessary. If the documents sent to you are in any way deficient, you must say so and insist that the solicitor commissioning your report rectifies the deficiency.

8.9   You should always be allowed access to the documentation which you deem it necessary to see in order properly to conduct your enquiries. If, for any reason, you are denied access to documents or material which you deem relevant to your enquiry, you should make immediate contact with the solicitor who commissioned your report. If that approach does not succeed, you should invite the solicitor to return to court to obtain an order from the judge for disclosure of the relevant documents to you.

8.10   Your letter of instruction should identify the relevant lay and professional people involved in the case and advise you of your right to talk to the other professionals engaged in it. This topic is covered in greater detail in Chapters 9 to 11.

Summary

8.11   It is of the utmost importance that you are properly and fully instructed and that you have access to all the material which is necessary for the proper preparation of your report. Your letter of instruction should be detailed and spell out clearly what is required of you. If it does not, or if you do not have access to material which you feel is necessary for the preparation of your report, you should not hesitate to say so and to take steps to ensure that you receive it.

9.1   How you go about the enquiries necessary for the writing of your report is, of course, a matter for you and outside the scope of this book. You must, of course, work to the brief given to you by the court (see Chapter 7), and the court will expect you to conduct your enquiries in conformity with the highest standards of your profession and with best professional practice. You should, moreover, bear the following three points in mind.

(1) Your report is likely to be the subject of careful scrutiny by the parties and by the court. You may be asked about the basis upon which you reached your conclusions, and the material available to you. You will therefore need to be able to demonstrate that your enquiries have been both careful and thorough.

(2) You should, of course, make a careful note of all interviews which you conduct in the course of your enquiries, and you should explain in your report what factors in particular have influenced you in reaching your conclusion.

(3) If you have had clinical experience of the child or children outside the immediate ambit of the litigation (for example if you are a paediatrician who has examined or treated the child prior to proceedings being taken) you should carefully review your notes before writing your court report and ensure that *all* your clinical material is available for inspection by the court and by other experts called upon to advise in the case. This includes (not an exhaustive list) all medical notes, hospital records, photographs, correspondence, and X-rays.

Summary

9.2   Within the framework which it has laid down for your enquiries, the court will not seek to inhibit the manner in which you conduct your enquiries. The court will, however, expect those enquiries to conform with the highest professional standards and best practice.

10.1   The practice in family proceedings is to encourage experts instructed to advise in a case to discuss it with other experts and professionals involved in the same case. Indeed, it has been said that experts instructed in a given case should always be invited to confer with each other prior to the final hearing both in order to inform their opinions and in an attempt to reach agreement or limit the issues.[1]

10.2   Contact between experts usually takes one or both of two forms:

(1) contact made between experts prior to their reports being written;
(2) a meeting of experts after reports have been completed.

10.3   There is in some quarters a misunderstanding of the position of experts in relation to contact with each other before reports are written. Some experts have appeared to be under the impression that they cannot talk to each other either because the papers are confidential or because they believe their instructions prohibit informal pre-hearing discussions between experts. One of the aims of this book is to eliminate this area of misunderstanding.

10.4   Your letter of instructions should contain a paragraph to the following effect:

> 'It is expected that you will have meetings with the parents, children (*where leave is given*), social workers and the guardian ad litem. You are also, of course, at liberty to discuss the case with any of the other experts instructed if you feel that would assist you in writing your report. It is, however, essential both to your role as an independent expert and to the parties' perception of your independent status, that when you do have informal discussions or correspondence with any of the professionals or the lay parties involved in the case, you should make an adequate note of all such discussions. You should also disclose the fact that you have had them when you write your report, and explain what influence, if any, such discussions have had upon your thinking and your conclusions.'[2]

10.5   What the court is anxious to prevent is any *unrecorded* informal discussions between particular experts which are either influential in, or determinative of, their views, and to which the parties to the proceedings (including perhaps other experts) do not have access.

10.6   It is therefore very important that you make an adequate note of any informal discussions you have with other experts in the case; that you set out in your report the fact that you have had such discussions; and, where those discussions are influential in your conclusions, that you disclose in your report the effect they have had on your conclusions. You may be asked to produce the note of any such discussion, either in advance of the hearing or in cross-examination.

10.7   If you are in any doubt about the propriety of any discussions which you have had or wish to have with other professionals in the case, you should seek advice from the solicitor who commissioned the report from you. The basic rule, however, is that within the framework laid down for you by the court you are free to conduct your enquiries in the manner which you believe to be most compatible with reaching the right conclusion and with your own professional and ethical standards. The corollary, however, is that you should explain your methodology in your report. You must also be able to defend it in court.

Summary

10.8   In making your enquiries for the purposes of your report, you are free to talk to other professionals in the case. You should, however, make a note of any such discussions, and refer to them in your report. If any such discussion has been influential in reaching your conclusion, you should say so in your report.

Notes

1   *Re S (Child Abuse Cases: Management)* [1992] 1 FCR 31; *Re C (Expert Evidence: Disclosure: Practice)* [1995] 1 FLR 204.

2   This paragraph is slightly different from the letter set out in the *Handbook of Best Practice in Children Act Cases* Children Act Advisory Committee (DOH, June 1997). The reason for this was that in *Re CB and JB* the author found that the version set out in the *Handbook* had been read by one of the experts in that case as prohibiting such discussions. The Expert Witness Group has also produced a draft letter of instruction for expert witnesses in children proceedings, which represents good practice. It reads as follows:

'**Contact with others**
You may wish to contact the solicitors of the other parties or the [parents] [carers] direct, to arrange meetings or for other practical reasons. Please feel free to do so. However, if in your contact with the solicitors you discuss any matter of

relevance, please inform us promptly and let us have copies of any reports or information given to you. **Please keep a careful record of all pertinent discussions with other experts or parties.** For ease of reference here are the names, addresses and telephone numbers of the most important contacts [*add whenever two or more experts are being instructed*: including in particular other expert[s] who have been instructed to consider the same issues. You may be required to attend a meeting with the[se] other expert[s] in order to establish agreed facts, common findings and areas of disagreement.]' (bold emphasis added)

Chapter Eleven

Meetings of Experts Directed by the Court

11.1 Meetings of experts arranged as a consequence of directions from the court are an important element in the process of preparation for a hearing.[1] At the same time, the obvious needs to be stated. Simply because there are experts in the case does not mean that a pre-hearing face-to-face meeting of experts is necessary.

11.2 Like every other procedural innovation, where experts' meetings are:

(a) necessary;
(b) set up with care; and
(c) conducted with intellectual rigour and discipline,

they can save an enormous amount of court time and reduce the costs of a case substantially. Where, however, such meetings are unfocused or badly conducted, they can obfuscate rather than clarify issues, thereby lengthening a case and increasing costs.

11.3 A meeting of experts is necessary only if there is something for you to discuss. If, on paper, you are all agreed, and if there is nothing in your reports which requires elucidation or amplification, there is no need for you to meet, and there should be no need for you to attend court to give oral evidence.

11.4 A meeting of experts is usually required, either because it is necessary to attempt to define or limit areas of disagreement, or because there are points in the case which require elucidation. The first question, therefore, is whether or not in such a case it is necessary for you to meet face to face.

11.5 In difficult child cases the experts are often widely geographically located. The courts recognise that it will not always be reasonable to expect you to find time to travel long distances in order to meet face to face. In many cases, you can agree or limit the areas of disagreement by telephone or fax. Sometimes telephone conferencing is sufficient, and serious consideration should be given to telephone conferencing in every case, provided always that any such conference has a proper agenda, is called to answer specific questions and is competently chaired and minuted.

11.6 Where a face-to-face meeting is arranged, sufficient time should be set aside for it so that the discussion does not take place under undue pressure of time. Equally, the meeting should not take place at the last minute, but should be so time-tabled as to enable the parties to have the opportunity to discuss the outcome and for the experts to reschedule their diaries if agreement is reached and they are not required to give evidence.

Which experts should attend a meeting?

11.7   In many cases, the essential issue is a factual one: for example, was the injury to the child accidental or non-accidental? If the latter, what was the mechanism and timing? What degree of force was required? In such cases, the expert evidence relevant to its elucidation is usually medical, and goes to causation and timing. In these circumstances, it is rarely helpful for such a meeting to be attended by psychologists and psychiatrists.

11.8   Lawyers seeking to organise a meeting of experts need always to give thought to the subject-matter to be addressed by the particular meeting, and the relevance of the disciplines of those invited to attend. This is a matter in which you plainly have a legitimate interest. If you think that a meeting is unnecessary, either because there is no issue between your colleagues and yourself, or because you think it unlikely to produce agreement or even a narrowing of the issues, you should explain your view to your colleagues and to the solicitor who commissioned your report.

11.9   A global meeting of experts from different disciplines may sometimes be appropriate if all the issues in a case are up for discussion and resolution. Such a situation is, however, in my experience, unusual.

11.10   Not only must great care be taken to ensure that experts' meetings are properly constituted to meet their particular objective, care must also be taken to ensure that, if separate meetings of different disciplines do take place in the context of a given case, those meetings are complementary to each other and have the same objective, namely the elucidation and, if possible, resolution of the relevant medical issues in the case.

11.11   It is therefore very important that you tell the solicitor who commissioned your report if you feel a meeting is unnecessary or that it is being called to address the wrong issues.

11.12   As part of the non-adversarial nature of the proceedings, the collection and marshalling of expert evidence in cases relating to children should be a co-operative process between the lawyers and the experts involved, irrespective of the source of their instructions. The issues in the case which require expert evidence must be identified and discussed in advance of the hearing. If agreement in relation to them is impossible, oral evidence will have to be called and tested and the judge will need to rule.

11.13   The object of experts' meetings, therefore, is to reduce or eliminate the need for contested oral expert evidence. This is often not sufficiently appreciated.

The conduct of the meeting

11.14   If meetings of experts are to succeed in achieving their objective of eliminating or narrowing areas of disagreement, it is essential that a strict intellectual discipline is applied to them. Meetings must therefore be focused carefully and clearly on the issues which you are to address.

11.15   Furthermore, the questions posed for you to answer must be clear and as straightforward as the subject-matter allows.

11.16   The format of an experts' meeting must ultimately be a matter for those attending it. However, there are certain basic guidelines which should always be observed.

11.17   There must be a clear agenda for the meeting. Specific questions for you to answer, or propositions for you to address, must be drawn up by the lawyers and presented to the meeting. The questions should be as concise and as clear as possible. They must be agreed between the parties' lawyers and given to the experts who are to attend the meeting in good time to enable you to prepare for it.

11.18   Because meetings of experts are perceived by the courts as a forensic tool whereby medical evidence addresses issues which are relevant to the court's decision, courts tend to the view that the meetings of experts which are most productive are those chaired by a lawyer.

11.19   The obvious choice for this role is the solicitor or counsel instructed by the guardian ad litem. Either of these lawyers should have a clear and unpartisan view of the issues in the case. It should, thus, normally be their responsibility to ensure that the agenda for the meeting addresses the issues upon which agreement is being sought or in respect of which the areas of agreement and disagreement need to be defined.

11.20   However, if lawyers are to chair meetings of experts, they must be sensitive to the different areas of expertise present at the meeting, and must ensure that they understand the weight which the doctors themselves give to each specialty. In a case involving complex medical issues, it may be sensible for the meeting to be chaired jointly by the child's lawyer and one of the doctors.

11.21   The court expects the lawyers for all of the parties to direct their minds to the questions which are to be posed to you. The questions should be as simple and as straightforward as the subject-matter allows. It is for the lawyers and, in particular, in the preparation for a meeting of experts, for the solicitor or counsel instructed by the guardian ad litem to distil the relevant issues in the case into a series of straightforward questions or propositions.

11.22   Ultimately, of course, if agreement cannot be reached as to the questions to be asked of the experts, the court will have to set the agenda. It should, however, normally be quite unnecessary to involve the court in this process.

11.23   Meetings of experts should be planned as a co-operative exercise between the lawyers and yourselves. The importance of your role in any such meeting is self-evident. You will therefore be asked to co-operate in making yourselves available for and participating in such meetings. If, however, you feel that a meeting is unnecessary, or has been called to address the wrong issues, or that the wrong disciplines have been invited, or that it is unlikely to achieve its objective, you should say so.

Minutes and statements of agreement and disagreement

11.24   It is of the greatest importance that a proper record is kept of all meetings of experts. This is usually best done by the guardian ad litem although, in complex cases, it may be appropriate to employ a shorthand writer. It is also important that the record of the meeting is produced and made available promptly to the participants and, if necessary, to the court.

11.25   It is, however, even more important that the results of the meeting itself are promptly distilled into a statement or similar document to which you can put your names and which thus acquires evidential status. Such a statement will be given to the judge who will have read it before you give evidence (assuming oral evidence is still necessary).

Summary

11.26   Meetings of experts pursuant to a direction from the court are an important forensic tool. They can save much time, by narrowing issues or by reaching agreement thereby rendering the oral evidence of experts unnecessary. However, a strict intellectual discipline must be applied to them. Whilst the logistics of setting up, conducting and reporting on such meetings are largely matters for the lawyers, experts have a vital role in ensuring that meetings are set up only when they are necessary and that they are productive.

Note

1   This chapter deals with meetings of experts designed to deal with evidential issues. You should be aware that, following the second conference organised by the President of the Family Division's Inter-disciplinary Committee (published as *Divided Duties* (Family Law, 1998)), a practice has developed in care proceedings whereby the court sometimes directs a meeting of relevant professionals to discuss the local authority's care plan. You may also be invited to such a meeting.

Chapter Twelve

Pre-hearing Conferences with Counsel and/or with the Solicitor who has Commissioned the Expert Report

12.1   If you have been instructed by only one of the parties, there is nothing improper or inappropriate about you being asked to attend a pre-hearing conference with counsel and/or the solicitor who has the conduct of that party's case in court. The purpose of that conference is to clarify and discuss your report; to bring you up to date with events in the case; and to discuss with you any material which has emerged since you wrote your report, notably perhaps, a report by one of your colleagues.

12.2   It is, however, bad practice in proceedings relating to children, bordering on professional impropriety, for lawyers to seek to 'coach' experts or invite you to form or modify particular opinions because they favour the client's case. If you are approached in this way, not only should you resist the approach firmly, but you should consider making a complaint to the High Court Family Division Liaison Judge for the circuit concerned (see Chapter 22 and Appendix 2) or to the professional body of the lawyers concerned. Such behaviour on the part of family lawyers cuts across the whole ethos of the independence of the expert, and the philosophy underlying the purpose of expert evidence in family proceedings.

12.3   You must be free to express opinions relevant to the child's welfare in a wholly disinterested way and without partisan pressure from lawyers.

12.4   Seeking to identify areas of agreement and disagreement in readiness for a court hearing should not be regarded as 'drawing battle lines'. Meetings of experts are a forensic tool, but gathering expert evidence is not to be regarded as an 'adversarial' process, rather as a co-operative exercise.

12.5   If disagreement remains, oral evidence will be required and the judge will have to resolve the issue. If there is total agreement between the experts:

(a) their attendance at court is likely to be unnecessary; and
(b) the agreement is likely to be determinative of the issues involved and, possibly, of the whole case. The purpose of a meeting of experts is to facilitate the legal process and assist the court. It should also focus the minds of the experts on the critical issues in the case.

Summary

12.6   Any attempt by lawyers to interfere with your independence or to persuade you to tailor your views to a particular standpoint is to be both deprecated and resisted.

Chapter Thirteen

Joint Instructions

13.1 It is quite common for individual experts in family proceedings to be jointly instructed by the parties to the proceedings. In care proceedings, this usually means that you will be instructed jointly by the solicitor acting for the child, the local authority solicitor and the parents' solicitor(s). The solicitor from whom you receive your letter of instruction will be the 'lead' solicitor for this purpose, and will usually be the solicitor instructed by the guardian ad litem on behalf of the child.

13.2 Apart from ensuring that you receive your letter of instruction and all the relevant documents, many of the principal functions of the lead solicitor in a case of joint instruction are largely administrative. One important task is to liaise with the other solicitors in the case; another is to ensure that all the solicitors in the case receive copies of all the correspondence which is generated as a consequence of your involvement.

13.3 The lead solicitor should be your first port of call if you require further documentation or information, or if you have a problem or query.

13.4 The lead solicitor should also be responsible for keeping you up to date with developments in the case, and for making the arrangements for any meeting of experts or professionals which you are invited to attend.

13.5 The lead solicitor will be responsible for ensuring, if you have to give oral evidence, that your evidence is time-tabled for a date and time which is convenient for you. The lead solicitor will also be responsible for ensuring that you are paid (see Chapter 23).

Reasons for joint instruction

13.6 There may be a number of reasons why the court has ordered a report from a single, jointly instructed expert. It may be, for example, that an intimate examination of the child in the case is required, or the court wants a psychiatrist to interview and assess the child. Courts are always anxious to limit the number of physical or psychiatric examinations which a child has to undergo, and so may permit only a single examination by one expert for the purposes of the case.

13.7 Another example of joint instruction is where a paediatric or psychiatric overview of the case is required. A third situation is where a discrete scientific issue arises, such as a hair or blood test for drugs, where joint instruction enables the cost of the exercise to be shared between the parties.

13.8 Joint instructions can, however, pose difficulties both for the expert instructed and for the lawyers in the case. This chapter will examine the benefits of joint instruction and some of the problems which arise.

The advantages of the jointly instructed expert

13.9 The fact that you have been jointly instructed means that you have either been chosen jointly by, or, at the very least are acceptable to, all the parties in the case. The process of joint instruction should thus tend to exclude from the legal process experts with views which tend strongly to favour one particular point of view. Furthermore, where the opinion of a jointly instructed expert is sufficiently authoritative and is accepted by the parties and the court, a great deal of court time and a large amount of legal costs can be saved.

13.10 If properly carried through, the joint instruction of a single expert may reduce the delay in the case being heard. There are, however, cases in which a party who disagrees with the conclusions of the jointly instructed expert (usually one or both of the child's parents) may be able to make out a case for a second opinion. Cases in which an expert is instructed jointly need therefore to be time-tabled with this possibility in mind so that, if a second opinion is required, there is time for it to be obtained without postponing the date fixed for the final hearing.

The disadvantages of joint instruction

13.11 To be the sole, jointly instructed expert in a difficult case places a considerable burden of responsibility on the expert concerned. The point on which you are being asked to advise may, you feel, be determinative of the child's future, yet there is nobody against whose opinion your diagnosis can be tested or with whom the burden of decision-making can be shared. You do not have a colleague from the same or a similar discipline instructed in the case with whom you can discuss your views. Your work is thus not the subject of peer review.

13.12   Although the burden of responsibility is substantial, you should remember that you do not decide the case: that is the judge's task. None the less, you should agree to accept a joint instruction only if you are wholly confident of your ability to undertake the brief given to you by the court.

13.13   As explained in para **13.10**, joint instruction can create difficulty and delay if the opinion of the jointly instructed expert is challenged by one of the parties who then wishes to seek a second opinion.

13.14   The legal status of the jointly instructed expert is not always clear. Whilst this is primarily a matter for the lawyers to discuss and agree amongst themselves, questions arise as to the extent to which it is proper for the jointly instructed expert to attend conferences with the lawyers for the individual parties, or to discuss the case with them. Difficulties can also arise in relation to the extent to which a jointly instructed expert can be challenged by way of cross-examination in the absence of any second opinion giving a different view.

13.15   Lay parties who commission an expert's report frequently see its purpose in terms of obtaining an opinion which is favourable to them. They may have similar expectations of a jointly instructed expert.

Guidelines for the jointly instructed expert witness

13.16   All the duties set out in Chapter 4 continue to apply to the jointly instructed expert witness. Subject to the terms of the brief given to you by the court, you have similar autonomy over the way you conduct your enquiries. The particular watchwords for the jointly instructed expert, however, are openness and even-handed communication.

13.17   Difficulties can particularly arise once you have written your report. What, for example, is the position if one party wishes to discuss your report with you, or wishes you to attend a conference without the other parties being present? Who can you talk to in the case about your report?

13.18   There is as yet no guidance from the courts on these questions. However, some points are reasonably clear. The first is that you will at all times exercise your professional and clinical judgment and behave in conformity with the ethical guidelines of your own professional body. That should not be difficult.

13.19   This leaves the question of your contact with the lawyers for the various parties. It is particularly in this area that difficulties can arise.

13.20   It is very important that the jointly instructed expert should not be perceived by any one of the parties as part of an opposing team. It is also very important for you to remember that the only documents or conversations in proceedings relating to children which are absolutely confidential and in respect of which disclosure cannot be ordered are those which cover the legal advice which the parties receive from their lawyers. This is called 'legal professional privilege'.

13.21   What is said to you during the course of your investigations, and what you say to others, is not covered by legal professional privilege. As a jointly instructed expert, it is simply not possible for you to have confidential discussions with one of the parties, the existence of which is not disclosed and the content of which is not recorded. In other words, where you are an expert witness in a child case there is no such thing as an 'off the record' or 'without prejudice' conversation.

Practical implications of joint instruction

13.22   There is nothing wrong in principle with a jointly instructed expert having conversations or meetings with the lawyers for one party, provided the fact of such contact and its content are made known to the other parties. Much will depend on the facts of the individual case, and the manner in which you feel it appropriate to address the questions on which you are asked to advise.

13.23   You may, for example, think it inappropriate in a particular case to attend a conference with counsel for one of the parties. On the other hand, in another case, you may take the view, after you have written your report, that it is necessary to have discussions with the parties or with their solicitors individually, or to talk through your conclusions with the parents with their solicitor present.

13.24   If you decide that conversations such as those described in the previous paragraph are appropriate, you should not hesitate to arrange them. You must, however, ensure that everything is done in the open and is transparent. Thus, both the fact that you have had such discussions, and, if relevant, their content and outcome must be known to the other parties and to the court.

13.25   Equally, in a particular case you may feel (and are entitled to require) that all queries arising out of your report should be raised with you and dealt with by you in writing so that you can be confident that each of the parties has received the same information contained in the same document. This is sometimes the safest course, and the one most likely to avoid misunderstandings and misinterpretation. If this is the approach you prefer, it is one for which you cannot be criticised.

13.26   The dangers of conversations between experts and lawyers outside the courtroom itself are self-evident. You run the risk of being misrepresented or misunderstood. You run the risk of giving the appearance of partiality. You lay yourself open to the suggestion that you have been inconsistent, and to cross-examination along the lines of:

> 'when you spoke to the parents' solicitor on the telephone, you said something quite different; you told them so and so, didn't you?'

13.27   You obviously do not want to put yourself in a position where your independence and professional integrity can be called into question, or from which misunderstandings may arise. Equally, you do not want to be accused of inconsistency, or of giving one message to one party and a different message to another.

13.28   You may consider it appropriate to arrange a meeting with all the parties' legal representatives to discuss your report and your conclusions. The advantage of this is that it provides a forum for questions and discussion in keeping with the inquisitorial role of the jointly instructed expert whose duty is to the child and to the court. Furthermore, it provides an opportunity for you as the jointly instructed expert to express your views on the validity, wisdom or otherwise of a second opinion being sought to test any of the conclusions you may have reached.

13.29   If you consider that a meeting such as that described in para **13.28** is appropriate and may be of value, whether or not it has been suggested by any of the legal advisers, you should invite the lead solicitor to make the arrangements.

13.30   It is, of course, quite improper for the lawyers for any party to seek to put pressure on you to change your opinion. This issue is discussed in Chapter 12. If, as the jointly instructed expert, you feel that is happening you should say so. It is not, however, improper for lawyers to put points to you which they feel you have overlooked or misinterpreted, or for them to invite you to reconsider your opinion in the light of fresh material. There is a clear distinction between these approaches.

13.31   If you do engage in correspondence with individual lawyers in the case, make sure that the lead solicitor arranges for your letters to be copied to the other parties (see para **13.2**).

13.32   If you have a telephone conversation with one of the parties' solicitors, you should make a written note of it as soon as possible. Alternatively, competent solicitors always make what they call 'an attendance note' of all relevant conversations they have during the conduct of a case. You can ask the solicitor to send you a copy of the attendance note made of any conversation with you. If this is done, and you disagree with the note, you should write to the solicitor in question, putting the record straight.

What to do if you are unhappy

13.33   If you are uneasy about a particular course of action which is proposed, or about attending a particular meeting, or having a particular conversation or discussion, the better course is, probably, not to do it. Alternatively, speak or write to the lead solicitor and ask their advice. If necessary, get that solicitor to obtain agreement for what you want to do from the other lawyers in the case. If what you want to do is controversial and of enough importance, ask the child's solicitor to set up a directions appointment before the judge, so that the judge can rule on the point.

13.34   Always remember that your function is to advise the court, not the parties. In a disputed case, the proper forum for the discussion of your report is the courtroom. The person with whom you are discussing the case outside the courtroom may later be cross-examining you on your report in the courtroom. That is not easy either for the lawyer or for you, and is another reason why you should be very cautious about having out of court discussions with the lawyers in the case apart from the lead solicitor.

Summary

13.35   Being a jointly instructed expert places a particularly heavy burden on you. Follow your professional judgment in making your enquiries. Be open and even handed in your dealings with the lawyers. Make a written note of any conversations you have with them. If the lawyers wish to discuss your report with you in advance of the hearing, or if you feel that you should, for example, take the opportunity to explain your conclusions to the parents with their lawyers present, you should feel free to do so. An alternative may be to invite all the lawyers in the case to a meeting at which you can explain your conclusions and answer questions. If you do have a conference with one of the parties and their lawyers, you must be able to justify the need for such a conference; you should ensure that the other parties know you are doing it, and that a proper record of what you say is made.

Chapter Fourteen

Where there are both Criminal and Children Act Proceedings

14.1   If you are a paediatrician, a radiologist or a pathologist, you may find yourself involved in a case in which a parent is facing criminal proceedings relating to a dead or seriously injured child, whilst the surviving siblings or the injured child are concurrently the subject of care proceedings under the Children Act 1989.

14.2   Similarly, in a case between parents where the issue is residence or contact, there may be an ongoing police/social services investigation into allegations of abuse against one of the parents.

14.3   There is, of course, no reason why you should not make a statement to the police as well as writing a report for the Children Act proceedings. Indeed, it is your duty to assist the police in their enquiries if you have medical information which is relevant to the injuries suffered by a child.

14.4   If, however, you have been instructed in the Children Act proceedings, you are not at liberty to disclose your report in those proceedings to the police without the permission of the court hearing the Children Act proceedings. This is because that report is confidential to those proceedings and cannot, without the permission of the court, be shown to any person or body not engaged in those proceedings.

14.5   The same rule also applies to any documents prepared for the purposes of the proceedings and filed with the court.

14.6   As is made clear in Chapter 2, however, whilst your report is confidential to the court, all relevant information obtained during the course of your enquiries must be shared in your report with the other parties and the court.

Accepting instructions in both sets of proceedings

14.7   If you are jointly instructed by the solicitors for the guardian ad litem, the parents and the local authority to advise the court in the Children Act proceedings, you should think very carefully before either making a statement to the police or accepting instructions on behalf of the defence in any concurrent criminal proceedings. The reason for this is that your information about the case will have come from the confidential material assembled for the Children Act proceedings, and your position as an independent expert in those proceedings may be compromised if you become actively involved in the criminal proceedings.

14.8   At the same time if, during the course of your enquiries in the Children Act proceedings you come across material which you believe to be of importance either to the prosecution or to the defence or, if, having completed your enquiries, you feel that your report should be seen by either the prosecution or the defence in the criminal proceedings, you should so advise the solicitor who commissioned your report (the solicitor instructed by the guardian ad litem in the example given). It will then be for that solicitor to apply to the court in order to obtain the leave of the judge in charge of the Children Act proceedings for your report or the relevant information to be disclosed.

Summary

14.9   There is no reason why an expert should not make statements both to the police and in the Children Act proceedings. However, knowledge acquired as a result of your instruction in the Children Act proceedings, or any report you write in those proceedings, can only be disclosed to the prosecution or to the defence with the leave of the court hearing the Children Act proceedings.

Chapter Fifteen

Writing the Report

15.1 There is no specific format required by the court for an expert's report.[1] The following suggestions touch only on topics which are particularly helpful to the court.

15.2 It is important that experts give a full curriculum vitae which explains the basis upon which they have the expertise to address the issues contained in the report. This can, for example, be done by appending the curriculum vitae to the report and by a reference in the text of the report.

15.3 Although the initial documents sent to you will have been listed in your letter of instruction, it is important that you should identify in your report all the documents you have seen. Either list them, or attach a copy of the letter of instruction to your report and, in the body of that report, list any additional documents which you have considered.

15.4 It is also important that you should set out all the other enquiries you have made. This will, of course, include any interviews you have conducted and any other material, such as videos, which you have seen. It will also include discussions with fellow experts and other professionals if these have occurred.

15.5 The court looks above all for clarity in presentation and in the conclusions reached. The court is concerned with:

(1) the issues it asked you to address;
(2) the material you have considered;
(3) the conclusions you have reached; and
(4) your reasons for reaching those conclusions.

15.6 Try to keep your report to a manageable length. Put yourself in the position of the judge who is reading your report for the first time, and who is interested in the matters set out in the preceding paragraph. If you need to set out the detail of interviews or material upon which your conclusions are based, put them in an appendix.

15.7 Your conclusions should, wherever possible, be clear and logically argued with the reasoning for them fully explained. Plain English should be used wherever possible, and complex or unusual medical terms explained. Use of double spacing, short, numbered paragraphs and sub-headings all make for easy reading. Please also write only on one side of each sheet of paper. Your report will be photocopied many times, and one of the easiest mistakes made in photocopying is for only one side of the page to be copied.

15.8   If, after writing your report, fresh information is made available to you, you must inform the commissioning solicitor in writing of any change which that information requires in your report. This should be done in a form which can be made available to the other parties and the court.

15.9   If you take the view that you have not had access to sufficient material to express a full opinion, you must say so in your report.

15.10   It is very important that you address the specific issues which you are asked to address and that you do not deviate into areas outside your expertise. If, however, you have not been asked to express an opinion on an issue which you feel is relevant, and it is one on which you can properly express an opinion, you should do so. Some letters of instruction will give you the opportunity to comment on 'any other issue which you feel to be relevant'.

Summary

15.11   There is no particular format for your report required by the court. It should, however, be written in plain English. It should be clear and well argued. It should identify all the material you have considered and relied upon. Its conclusions should also be clear and well reasoned.

Note

1   Useful guidelines for the structure of an expert's report are to be found in the *Expert Witness Pack* produced by the Expert Witness Group (published by Jordans), and in Tufnell 'Psychiatric Court Reports in Child Care Cases: What Constitutes Good Practice' published in the Association of Child Psychology and Psychiatry Review and Newsletter (1993) vol 15, pp 219–224. There is also an excellent chapter and model report by Dr Frank Bamford in *Recent Advances in Paediatrics*, ed T J David (Churchill Livingston, 1994). See also the suggested reading list in Appendix 1, particularly Plotnikoff and Woolfson *Reporting to Court under the Children Act (A Handbook for Social Services)* (DOH, 1996).

Chapter Sixteen

Changing your Opinion

16.1 If, as a result of fresh information received after you have written your report, you wish to revise your opinion, not only are you free to do so, but you owe a positive duty to the court to do so, and to advise the court of the reasons for your change of stance.

16.2 Experts whose minds are open and who change their opinions appropriately on the receipt of fresh information are respected by the court. Provided your original opinion was soundly based, and provided there is good reason for any change of opinion, your change of stance is unlikely to be criticised by the court, although you may have to defend it in cross-examination.

16.3 It is therefore extremely important that your original opinion should be soundly based and cogently argued. It is always worth bearing in mind that although your report is written for the court and for the child, your views inevitably have a considerable impact on the lay parties to the proceedings. Particularly in disputed cases where the allegation is non-accidental injury, an unsound or untenable position taken by an expert one way or the other which then has to be revised may well be difficult for a lay party to accept. This is particularly the case where the original opinion appears to exclude abuse or exonerates an alleged participant.

16.4 You may change your opinion as a consequence of a meeting with your colleagues of the type described in Chapter 11. You should, of course, approach a meeting of experts with your mind open to the arguments of your colleagues and to the discussion which takes place. If you find those arguments properly persuasive and as a consequence change your opinion for good reason, you will need to ensure that the reasons for your change of stance are properly minuted; but, for the reasons already given, you are unlikely to be subject to any criticism from the court.

16.5 It is, however, equally important that any reasons for a change of stance are transparent. It should go without saying that you should not be bullied or coerced by your colleagues into a change of stance for reasons of convenience or any other inappropriate or improper motive. As has already been said, the courts value your independence and integrity. Any attempt, from whatever source, to tamper with that integrity is to be deprecated.

Summary

16.6 Experts who change their opinions for good reason on the receipt of fresh information are respected by the court rather than criticised. However, if you change your opinion, you should always explain why you have done so.

Chapter Seventeen

Preparing for Court

Logistics

17.1   Where the medical evidence is unanimous on the point or points which the experts have been asked to address, the presence of any of the medical witnesses to give oral evidence is unlikely to be justified. If you are asked to attend court in these circumstances, you should query with the commissioning solicitor why you are being asked to attend and, in particular, whether your attendance is being required by the judge.

17.2   In the past, the legal profession often treated the convenience of expert witnesses with a casualness which was both unconducive to any concept of mutual co-operation and likely to reinforce the reluctance which many of you have about giving evidence in court.

17.3   Good practice now requires lawyers to recognise that expert witnesses are busy people with many professional calls upon their time, and that giving evidence in court is both time-consuming and takes you away from your clinical duties and other important professional commitments.

17.4   A number of recent decisions by judges are designed to consult the convenience of expert witnesses and to try to ensure that your time is not wasted. Good practice now requires:

(1)   that a date and time for your evidence is fixed substantially in advance of the hearing, so that you can fit it into your other professional commitments;

(2)   that, if your oral evidence is not required, you are notified as far in advance of the hearing as possible so that you do not find yourself travelling to court only to find that you are not, after all, needed;

(3)   that the lawyers give the judge an estimate of how long you are likely to be in the witness-box so that your evidence can be time-tabled, and you can fix other professional commitments around it. In particular, every effort should be made to ensure that your evidence does not exceed the time allotted for it so that you do not have to come back on another day to finish it.

17.5   Where you have been asked to attend court at a particular time on a particular day, judges hearing cases under the Children Act will normally interpose your evidence at that point, even if that means interrupting another witness. Alternatively, expert evidence in a contested case may be arranged so that experts from similar disciplines can listen to each other's evidence.

17.6 You need to be proactive in ensuring that suitable arrangements have been made for your evidence. Your secretary or somebody on your behalf should be in regular touch with the solicitor who has commissioned your report to ensure in particular:

(1) that the case is being heard on the dates fixed for it;
(2) that your evidence is still needed;
(3) that a firm date and time has been set aside for your evidence;
(4) that you are up to date with any recent developments in the case;
(5) that there are no additional documents which have come to light since you wrote your report and which you have not seen;[1] and
(6) that all the relevant documents referred to in your report are before the court.

Summary

17.7 The lawyers and the court should ensure that your oral evidence is fixed for a date and time which is convenient for you and that it does not exceed the time set aside. You need to play your part in ensuring that you attend court only if it is strictly necessary for you to do so.

Note

1 See *Re G, S and M (Wasted Costs)* [2000] 1 FLR 52, in which I ordered a member of the bar to pay the costs incurred in requiring an expert witness to return on another occasion after she had been shown documents for the first time when giving evidence, and required time to read and consider them.

Chapter Eighteen

Witness Summonses (formerly known as Subpoenas)

18.1   Following the introduction of the Civil Procedure Rules 1998 the term 'subpoena' has been replaced for all purposes by the term 'witness summons'. A witness summons is an order to attend the court on a given date to give evidence under pain of being in contempt of court and liable to be punished if you do not attend. It is a document which has to be obtained from the court by one of the parties and it is served personally on you.

18.2   Nothing is more counter-productive to good relations between expert witnesses and lawyers than for the expert witness to be served with a witnesses summons, particularly if no notice of an intention to issue such a summons has been given to you. This is particularly the case if the summons requires you to attend court at very short notice or on a given day and 'each following day of the hearing until the court tells you that you are no longer required'.

18.3   If a case is properly managed, it should only be necessary to have an expert witness attend court pursuant to a witness summons in one of three circumstances:

(1) where the witness personally requests a witness summons to be issued;
(2) where there is evidence that the witness has not co-operated in making arrangements to come to court to give evidence; or
(3) where the interests of the child require the attendance of the witness as a matter of urgency and in circumstances which the court determines are sufficient to override other professional commitments which the witness may have.

18.4   There are certain professionals, such as health visitors and some therapists, who require to be ordered to attend court and give evidence under the compulsion of a witness summons so that they can avoid giving the impression that they are willing parties to what they or their clients may perceive as a breach of a confidential relationship. Sometimes, a professional witness may ask to be served with a witness summons as a protection against criticism for failing to be in two places at the same time.

18.5   Where it is suggested that the witness has not co-operated, the issue of a witness summons should none the less be regarded as a matter of last resort and evidence should be available to the court of non co-operation before a witness summons is issued.

18.6 If you are served with a witness summons without warning or prior consultation, you should immediately seek an explanation from the solicitor who commissioned your report or who applied for the summons. If there is a reasonable explanation for the summons and your evidence is required, it should be possible for you to negotiate a date and time at which you can attend court.

18.7 If the summons requires you to attend the court the next morning, and is served out of hours, or if it is served in other circumstances which make it impossible for you to make immediate contact with the solicitor who commissioned your report, you should obey the summons if you possibly can, and complain to the judge either in person or later in writing about the way you have been treated. If you cannot attend court in obedience to the summons, you should ensure that your secretary or somebody on your behalf communicates immediately with the court to explain why you cannot attend. It should then be possible for you to agree a time to attend if your evidence is really necessary. A properly organised case should, however, never reach this stage.

Summary

18.8 If the system has operated properly, a witness summons should be necessary only if you require one to be issued for any reason. You do, however, need to ensure that you remain in contact with the lawyers who are making arrangements for your attendance at court in order to avoid any misunderstandings. If you are served with a summons inappropriately and you cannot negotiate a time to attend court, you should obey the summons if you possibly can, and should protest. If you cannot obey it, ensure that you communicate with the court to explain why.

Chapter Nineteen

What Happens at and in Court: Introduction

19.1 Many expert witnesses find the courtroom a hostile environment. This ought not to be the case in family proceedings relating to children.

19.2 Cross-examination, in particular, is perceived by some experts as a gladiatorial combat in which the lawyers make the rules and change them as they go along. This is a misconception.

19.3 You are giving evidence to assist the judge reach a difficult decision about the welfare of a child. As His Honour Judge Harold Wilson put it in one of the cases:

> 'The game of adversarial litigation has no point when one is trying to deal with fragile and vulnerable people like small children.'[1]

19.4 Proceedings relating to children are highly emotive for the parties engaged in them. As a consequence, they need to be conducted in court in as calm and studied an atmosphere as possible. All the witnesses should be treated with courtesy by the judge and the lawyers. It is the task of both the judge and the lawyers to create and to maintain the appropriate atmosphere for calm and rational investigation of the issues.

19.5 It is the task of the judge to ensure fair play and to prevent irrelevant or hostile cross-examination. Cross-examination should go to issues, not personalities. All witnesses are entitled to be treated fairly and with courtesy, even, perhaps particularly, when their views are being rigorously tested.

19.6 Whatever the reason you have been summoned to court, you should be told in advance by the solicitor who has commissioned your report why you are being asked to attend, and the issues in the case which you will be specifically asked to address in your oral evidence. If you are not given this information in good time, make sure that you ask for it before you come to court. Any last minute queries can be resolved in a short conference at court with the lawyer calling you to give evidence.

Summary

19.7   The courtroom is not your normal workplace, and you may feel nervous or uneasy about attending court and giving evidence. Both the lawyers and, in particular, the judge should, however, ensure that you are fairly and courteously treated, and that the proceedings are conducted in a calm and rational atmosphere.

Note

1   *Oxfordshire County Council v M and Another* [1994] Fam 151 at 158.

At Court: Who can you Talk to?

20.1   You arrive at court. You should have been told the name of the judge and the number of the court before you arrive. Are there any rules about who you can talk to before you actually give your evidence?

20.2   Expert witnesses are often unsure about whether or not it is proper for them to talk to counsel or solicitors or any of the parties outside the doors of the court and immediately prior to giving oral evidence. The following suggestions are offered as guidance: ultimately, it must be a matter for you and the exercise of your professional judgement.

20.3   If it has been necessary for you to come to court, the likelihood is that this is because your report remains in contention with one or more of the parties, and your oral evidence is required for that reason. It follows that, if there are to be further discussions about your evidence outside court, there must be a good reason for any such discussions.

20.4   Your report will usually have been commissioned by one of the parties. It is therefore perfectly proper for you to have a conference with the lawyers representing the party who commissioned your report before you go into court. The purpose of such a conference will be to ensure that you are up to date with developments both in and out of court; to ensure that you have seen all relevant documents; and for the lawyer who is calling you to give evidence to discuss with you what issues will be addressed during the first part of the questioning, your examination-in-chief, which is conducted by that lawyer.

20.5   Where you have been instructed by one party only, you should not talk to the lawyers for any of the other parties about the case without either obtaining the agreement of the lawyers for the party who commissioned your report, or at the very least telling them that this is what you propose to do. There must, moreover, be a good reason for any such discussions. Bear in mind that the lawyer to whom you are then talking will shortly be cross-examining you in court, and may wish to make use of any discrepancy between what you have said outside and what you say in the witness-box.

20.6   Remember also that you are there to give evidence to the judge, not to discuss the case with the lawyers.

20.7   Where you have been instructed by the parties jointly the safest course is to adopt the same approach. Thus it would be perfectly proper for you to have a short conference with the lawyers for the lead party (usually the lawyers instructed by the guardian ad litem) before giving evidence, but it would be prudent to talk to any of the other parties' lawyers about the case only if there is a particular reason to do so and with the agreement of the lawyers for the lead party.

20.8   In some cases, the commissioning party may abandon reliance on the expert he or she has instructed. This usually occurs when you produce a report which is unhelpful to the case of the commissioning party. In such a case, if you are required to attend court, you may be called by one of the other parties, or you may be called by the judge, to enable each of the parties to cross-examine you. If this occurs, you should be informed in advance either by the solicitor who commissioned the report or by the solicitor instructed by the guardian ad litem.

20.9   It is generally undesirable for you to have any conversation with any of the lay parties to the proceedings at court prior to giving evidence unless there is a good reason to do so and there is general agreement that you should talk to the party in question.

20.10   If you feel in difficulty about whom you should or should not talk to about the case immediately before giving evidence, the best course is to speak only to the lawyers who are going to call you to give evidence.

20.11   Nothing, however, should prevent you exchanging the normal courtesies with the parties and their lawyers outside the court. If you have not met the parents before, you may wish to be introduced to them. If you think it would be helpful to speak to them, or to their lawyers, about the case – perhaps to explain your conclusions to them – there is no reason why you should not do so if they are willing to talk to you and their lawyers agree.

20.12   In a nutshell, however, if the system is operating properly, you should arrive at court in time to be brought up to date by the lawyers who commissioned your report. You should then go at once into the witness-box.

Summary

20.13   When arriving at court it is perfectly in order for you to have a short conference with the lawyers for the party who commissioned your report and who are calling you to give your evidence-in-chief. You should discuss the case with the other lawyers or any of the parties only if there is a particular reason to do so and if all the lawyers in the case agree that it is appropriate for you to do so. There is nothing to prevent the usual courtesies being exchanged outside the door of the court.

Chapter Twenty-One

Giving Evidence

21.1 This chapter is divided into the following sections as follows:

(1) Address the judge
(2) Taking the oath or affirming
(3) Evidence-in-chief
(4) Identify the lawyers
(5) Cross-examination
(6) Re-examination
(7) Where your evidence spans an adjournment or there is a break while you are giving evidence
(8) Questions from the judge

21.2 Your evidence will be divided into three parts:

(1) examination-in-chief;
(2) cross-examination; and
(3) re-examination.

This chapter deals with each in turn. It begins, however, with a point of general importance which is often not fully appreciated by witnesses.

Address the judge

21.3 Witnesses give evidence to the judge or magistrates, not to the barrister or solicitor asking the questions. It is, therefore, both correct and courteous to address the judge when giving evidence. High Court Judges are called either 'My Lady' or 'My Lord' according to gender: Circuit Judges, Recorders and Assistant Recorders are called 'Your Honour'. The Chair of a Lay Bench is addressed either as 'Sir' or 'Madam' according to gender. If in doubt about how to address the tribunal, ask the lawyer calling you to give your evidence-in-chief before you go into the witness-box.

21.4 Addressing your answers to the judge or magistrates is not only courteous and correct; it has two further advantages. First, it enables you to develop a rapport with the judge, and thus prevents you from becoming engaged in a lawyer-led discussion in which the lawyer asking the questions inevitably dictates their substance and the pace at which they are asked. Secondly, it gives you fractionally more time to think about what you are saying.

21.5 Most courtrooms are so designed that in order to look at the cross-examiner, the witness has to turn away from the judge. Although it is difficult, you should always try to turn back to face the judge when giving your answer. This process emphasises that you are giving evidence to the judge, not conducting a private discussion with the lawyer asking the questions.

21.6 You should always bring your notes and any relevant files with you. Alternatively, you should check in advance that the court has all the relevant material before it. Nothing irritates the court more than witnesses who do not have with them vital pieces of information contained in a file which is not in court. Your report of what was said by a person whom you have interviewed may well be challenged. You are likely to have made a contemporaneous note of your interview with that person. You may be asked if you made a note and, if so, what it said. If you do not have your notes with you, you immediately create a poor impression and your professionalism is devalued.

Taking the oath or affirming

21.7 When you go into the witness-box, you will be asked by the court usher whether you wish to take the oath or whether you wish to affirm. The oath is a promise, on the Bible or other religious text, to tell the truth. Affirmation is a promise to do so. You will be asked to read the relevant words from a printed card the usher will give you.

21.8 An affirmation carries identical weight to the oath, and you have an absolute right to affirm if you wish to, for example because you have no religious beliefs. If you wish to avoid any mix-up or hesitation, either tell the usher before you go into court how you wish to take the oath, or get one of the lawyers to do so.

Examination-in-chief

21.9 Examination-in-chief is the first part of your evidence, and is conducted by the lawyer for the party who commissioned your report. You will be asked to identify yourself and to give your professional address and qualifications. You will then be asked to identify your report, which you will probably have loose, but which will also be in a bundle of documents being used by the court, a copy of which should be in the witness-box.

21.10   Technically, the lawyer calling you should not ask you any leading questions unless they are uncontroversial. A leading question is one which either suggests a particular answer or contains the answer within the question. You may, however, sometimes hear one of the lawyers telling the lawyer conducting your examination-in-chief not to 'lead' on a controversial point, or the judge might intervene in the same way.

21.11   The judge will have read your report in advance of your appearance in court. There is therefore no need for you to repeat the contents of your report in your oral evidence. The purpose of your examination-in-chief is to clarify any part of your report which the lawyer calling you may not think is clear, and to invite you to comment on developments since your report was written. This may include evidence which has been given in court before you were called to give evidence.

21.12   All these matters should have been discussed with you outside court, and you should not be taken by surprise. Proceedings under the Children Act are heard 'in chambers', that is to say in private, and unless you have asked or been asked to sit in on other evidence, you are unlikely to have heard any of the other witnesses in the case. However, if you and a colleague are both giving evidence on the same point, you may be invited to remain in court for each other's evidence.

21.13   Except in the most complex cases, your evidence-in-chief is likely to be short. You will then be cross-examined by each of the other lawyers in the case.

Identify the lawyers

21.14   Particularly in care proceedings, where there are usually several parties, you may feel at a disadvantage when you go into court if you do not know the name of the lawyer asking you questions, or the perspective from which the questions are coming.

21.15 If you do feel this way, you should ask the lawyer who is calling you to give evidence to identify for you the lawyers acting for the other parties. This can either be done before you go into court or when you are in the witness-box. You will then be able to refer to them by name in court if you wish to, and will know the perspective from which the questions they are asking you originate. Good lawyers will often volunteer this information before they begin to ask you questions.

Cross-examination

21.16 There are many misapprehensions and much mythology surrounding cross-examination. Its purpose, with lay witnesses, is to test credibility. With expert witnesses, its purpose is to test the validity of the opinions you have expressed. You must therefore expect a rigorous examination of your conclusions and of your methodology. Cross-examination, if well conducted, is helpful to the judge and, if your report is well written, your conclusions sound and your methodology appropriate, you have nothing to fear. It is idle to pretend that cross-examination is a pleasurable process, but you may find intelligent questions stimulating and sometimes even helpful.

21.17 Cross-examination should always be courteous. In criminal cases, where there is a jury present, judges tend to be less interventionist for fear of giving the appearance of bias. Family proceedings are quasi-inquisitorial in nature, and the judge should intervene if the cross-examination becomes personal or offensive.

21.18 As has already been explained in Chapter 2, in family proceedings the court's enquiry into the welfare of the child is 'non-adversarial'. This does not, of course, mean that contentious issues of fact and opinion do not arise in proceedings relating to children, and will not arise during your evidence. If you have expressed firm opinions, you must expect to be firmly challenged on them.

21.19 However, cross-examination, particularly of an expert witness, should always go to issues, not personalities, and your credibility as an expert should only ever be in issue if you have stepped outside the bounds of your expertise, gone inappropriately beyond your instructions, or adopted a methodology for the preparation of your report which is open to criticism. Even then, the cross-examination should be directed to the validity of your conclusions and the consequences for the children concerned in the case of any error you may have made.

21.20 If you are anxious about cross-examination, remember that you will almost always know more about your subject than the lawyer asking the questions, or the judge listening to you. On the other hand, the lawyer knows what the next question will be.

Four golden rules

21.21 There are four golden rules.

(1) Always answer the question put to you. That sounds easy, but it is not. Do not seek to evade the question, or answer what you think will be the next question. If you cannot answer the question, perhaps because it takes you outside the ambit of your expertise, say so.

(2) Take your time. Do not allow the questioner to rush you. Never hesitate to ask for time to think if you are asked a particularly difficult question. The judge wants your carefully considered opinion.

(3) Try to keep your answers short and to the point. The judge wants answers, not a lecture.

(4) Never try to score points or get into an argument with the questioner. Doing so is inconsistent with your role as an expert witness and is unlikely to help the judge. The judge wants your objective professional opinion. It is for the lawyers to argue the case.

21.22 If you are asked to give a 'yes or no' answer to a question which you feel requires qualification, either say: 'the answer to your question is "yes" (or "no" as the case may be), but that needs to be qualified by …' (you can then provide the qualification). Alternatively, if the question simply cannot be answered 'yes' or 'no', say so. 'I am very sorry, My Lord/Lady/Your Honour, but I simply cannot give a yes or no answer to that question. It all depends on …' (then explain your reasons).

21.23   Since the judge's objective will be to keep the atmosphere in court calm and rational, try not to become exasperated if the lawyers' questioning demonstrates a fundamental ignorance of the topic under discussion. Once again, the best course is to talk to the judge. The more in sorrow than in anger approach is always to be preferred: 'My Lord/Lady/Your Honour, I think the question Mr/Ms X has asked demonstrates a misunderstanding of the position . . .' (you can then explain the misapprehension).

21.24   If you feel the cross-examination is repetitious or offensive, once again address the judge. 'My Lord/Lady/Your Honour, I think I have already answered that question, but if you wish I will go over it again'. If you think the cross-examiner is implying something offensive, say something like: 'My Lord/Lady/Your Honour, I am not clear about the implication behind the question but if it is being suggested that I have misunderstood the nature of the child's injuries, I disagree'.

21.25   Never hesitate to make appropriate concessions to the cross-examiner; experts who are willing to make proper concessions are always more respected by a judge than those who stick to their opinions through thick and thin.

21.26   You should always provide an opinion, not an argument. The expert who is perceived as arguing a case tends to lose objectivity and gives the impression of partiality.

21.27   Cross-examination should not be an ordeal. It is healthy for every profession to have its opinions and its methodology tested by outsiders, and there is no reason why you should not find cross-examination stimulating and helpful to you in clarifying your thought processes and conclusions.

21.28   Remember always, the golden rule of expert evidence: you are in court to help the judge reach a conclusion about the child. The case is not about you and, as has already been stated, you should not be subject to any personal attack unless you have broken the rules in some specific way or fallen below the high standards of your profession.

Re-examination

21.29   The purpose of re-examination, which is conducted by the lawyer who conducted your examination-in-chief, is to clarify points made in cross-examination. (In adversarial litigation its object is to repair the damage done in cross-examination.) For the lawyer, re-examination is difficult, because the rule is that leading questions are not allowed. This is because suggesting an answer to a witness who has said something different in cross-examination rarely has any evidential value. Many lawyers do not attempt re-examination, particularly with a competent expert witness.

Where your evidence spans an adjournment or there is a break while you are giving evidence

21.30   The normal rule is that if there is a break in the proceedings while you are in the middle of your evidence, you should not talk to anybody about the case until your evidence is concluded. The obvious reason for this is the risk that your evidence may be contaminated or influenced by something said to you outside the courtroom. If, for any reason, you want the rule relaxed, you should ask the judge before the court breaks whether it is in order for you to talk to a particular person.

21.31   For the same reasons, once your evidence is concluded, you should not talk to any of your colleagues or any of the other witnesses about the case or your evidence until their evidence is concluded. Always bear in mind that unauthorised publication of information relating to proceedings in chambers is a contempt of court.

Questions from the judge

21.32   The judge is quite likely to ask you questions either during the course of your evidence or when the lawyers have concluded. Lay magistrates are far less likely to do so, and their questions will come through the chair.

Summary

21.33 Your evidence will consist of taking the oath, examination-in-chief, cross-examination and, possibly, re-examination. You may take the oath or affirm. It is courteous, as well as likely to help put you at your ease, if the lawyers for the various parties identify themselves. This can either be done in court, or you can ask the lawyer who is calling you to give evidence to identify the other lawyers in the case. Do not talk to anyone about the case during breaks in your evidence or until the case is over.

You have come to court to give evidence to the judge. Talk to the judge, not to the lawyer asking you questions. And always bring your file.

So far as cross-examination is concerned, remember that you are the expert and that everybody in court knows less about the subject matter of your evidence than you do, apart from your fellow experts. Answer the question. Do not lose your temper. If you want time to think, ask for it. Do not engage in an argument with the lawyer cross-examining you. Make concessions where appropriate. Give the court your opinion, not an argument in favour of one side rather than the other.

Chapter Twenty-Two

Feedback and Complaints

22.1   You should not hesitate to ask for feedback at the end of the case after the evidence has been completed. This can either take the form of a letter from the commissioning solicitor or, where the judgment of the court has been transcribed, a copy of the judgment. Leave to disclose the judgment to you should, however, be obtained from the court.

22.2   You may feel you have been badly treated in a number of ways. You may have been inadequately instructed; you may not have received all the relevant documents; the parties may not have co-operated with you; you may feel that the lawyers or the judge have been discourteous; you may have been given no notification, or only very late notification, that your evidence was no longer required; you may have been called to court unnecessarily or kept hanging about at court; the time set aside for your evidence may not have been sufficient; you may have been served at home with a witness summons. These are only examples – there may be others.

22.3   Each circuit has a Family Division Liaison Judge (FDLJ), one of whose functions is to ensure the smooth running of family proceedings on the circuit. Any complaint should, in the first instance, be addressed to the FDLJ for the circuit concerned. The names of the FDLJs and identification of their circuits are set out in Appendix 2.

Summary

22.4   Ask for feedback. If you have good cause to feel you have been badly treated, you should not hesitate to say so. Inter-disciplinary co-operation in proceedings under the Children Act is a continuing process. Each discipline needs to learn from the other. Lawyers and judges expect a great deal of experts: the legal profession therefore needs to know what is acceptable to you in the way you are treated and what is not.

Chapter Twenty-Three

Payment of Experts' Fees and Charges

23.1   You will wish to be paid for the work you undertake whether you are instructed as an expert witness or because you have a direct clinical involvement with a patient involved in the proceedings. This will include being paid for time spent in reading and considering papers and documents, undertaking interviews or examinations, discussions and meetings with others (where appropriate and necessary), corresponding with solicitors, preparing and writing reports, attending at court and travelling.

23.2   In family proceedings, it is the solicitors who instruct expert or other professional witnesses who pay them as a general rule. When you accept instructions from a solicitor to act as an expert witness with a view to providing advice or a report in connection with proceedings, you enter into a contractual relationship with that solicitor, his firm or employer. It is an implied term of any such contract that you are entitled to be paid reasonable fees and expenses for the work you properly undertake in pursuance of the contract.

23.3   The contractual relationship between you and the solicitor is not dependent on how or by whom the solicitor is paid. It is likely that, in the majority of family cases in which you are instructed, the solicitor will be acting for a client under a Legal Representation certificate and will be paid his costs and disbursements (which will include your fees) by the Legal Services Commission. However, in some cases you will be asked to act by local authorities or by solicitors whose clients are funding the proceedings on a private client basis.

23.4   On 1 April 2000, the Legal Aid Board was replaced by the Legal Services Commission[1] which is responsible for establishing and maintaining the Community Legal Service. As part of the Community Legal Service, the Commission will manage the Community Legal Service Fund which has replaced the civil legal aid scheme with which you may have been familiar. Some of the familiar terminology in relation to legal aid has changed. The 'legal aid certificate' has been replaced by a 'Legal Representation certificate' for a party involved in proceedings before the court.

23.5 The changes have significant implications for lawyers in relation to the funding of the cases in which they are instructed to act. The funding of Legal Representation is subject to much tighter control than previously. High cost cases where the actual or likely costs under the certificate exceed £25,000 will be dealt with by the Legal Service Commission's 'Special Cases Unit'. Part of the requirements falling on lawyers dealing with such high cost cases will include having 'a costed overall case plan'.

23.6 Whilst these changes may not directly impact on the work you may be required to undertake within the court context, they do have some implications for you in relation to the requirement of being able to provide an estimate of charges to be made for the work to done by you and how you will be paid. The most important factor for you to establish before agreeing to accept instructions or undertaking any work, whether in a high cost case or under a certificate for Legal Representation, is what, if any, cost limitation exists in relation to the work to be done.

23.7 It is important that you should carefully consider the terms of your contractual agreement with the solicitors before you accept instructions and start work. The key issues to consider are how much will you be paid, when will you be paid and what limitation there might be on the amount you can charge for the work you will have to do.

23.8 You should have a written agreement with the solicitor which sets out details of your charging rates on an hourly basis for different types of work which you may have to undertake. The agreement can be in either a separate formal document or a letter.

23.9 A solicitor wishing to instruct you should, as a matter of good practice before he does so, ask you to provide details of your hourly charging rates for different aspects of your work such as interviewing or examining the client, preparation, writing the report, attending meetings, travelling, waiting at court and engaged in court. You should expect to be asked to provide an overall written estimate of how much you consider your total fees will be for the work you are being asked to undertake in any case which is funded by the Community Legal Service.

23.10   There are four reasons as to why this information is required.

(1) So that the solicitor can advise his client of the possible cost liability being incurred if you are to be instructed. Solicitors are required to inform their clients of expenditure which is to be incurred by instructing an expert.[2] This applies, broadly speaking, to both private paying clients and those funded by the Community Legal Service (CLS).

(2) All Legal Representation certificates issued contain 'costs limitations' which limit the total amount of costs and disbursements payable to the solicitors. The costs limitations can be extended by the Legal Services Commission provided application is made before the costs are incurred. Frequently, you will be asked for an estimate of your fees and charges in writing to enable the solicitor to seek such an extension.

(3) If the solicitor's client is receiving Legal Representation from the Community Legal Service Fund, the information may be required so that the solicitor can obtain a 'prior authority' from the Legal Services Commission which is a means of guaranteeing that the expert's fees will be paid within the limitation of any authority given.

(4) The court also requires the information so that it can assess whether or not the fees likely to be incurred are reasonable within the overall context of the proceedings.

23.11   There will occasionally be cases where it is not possible to give an accurate indication of how much your fees will be because it is not possible to predict how much time it will take to do the work. In such a case, you will still need to give some estimate but should make it clear that this figure may need to be revised. You should indicate what the uncertain factors are which may give rise to the need for revision. The solicitor will proceed to seek a 'prior authority' or increase in the 'cost limitation' on the Legal Representation certificate based on the information provided. If it becomes apparent that your fees will exceed your original estimate, you must inform the solicitor so that he can make an application to further extend the 'prior authority' or 'cost limitation'. It is important to note that this must be done before the conclusion of the proceedings and preferably before the additional work is undertaken by you. Failure to do so may result in the solicitor quite properly refusing to make any payment over and above your original estimate. This underlines the importance of keeping a proper running record of the time you may expend dealing with a case and being aware of the costs being incurred.

23.12   When you will be paid depends on the terms you agree with the solicitor. There is no term, implied or otherwise, that you have to wait until the solicitor has been paid before you can be paid. As with suppliers of other services, it is likely that the terms you would include in any agreement to accept instructions will be that you should be paid within 30 days of delivering your invoice in respect of the work done.

23.13   Solicitors may wish to agree different terms of payment with you. This is particularly likely to arise in relation to cases funded by the CLS. In a CLS-funded case dealt with in the family proceedings (magistrates') court, the solicitor's costs and disbursements will be assessed and authorised for payment by the Legal Services Commission. Your fees are treated as a disbursement. It is the Legal Services Commission that will determine whether the fees you have charged are reasonable. Provided that the solicitor has obtained a 'prior authority' in respect of your fees and they are within the limit set by that 'prior authority' then no difficulty should arise in relation to any question of the amount of the payment.

23.14   In cases which proceed in the county court or the High Court, the amount of the solicitor's costs and disbursements payable under his client's Legal Representation certificate are determined by the court by a process called 'detailed assessment' ('detailed assessment' is the term now used arising from changes made by the Civil Procedure Rules effective from April 1999 to replace the term 'taxation of costs'). This means that the amount of costs and disbursements incurred and claimed for payment is examined by the court to determine whether it is appropriate and reasonable. The court has the power to reduce the costs and disbursements claimed if the assessing officer is of the opinion that the hourly rates charged or amounts claimed are excessive or unreasonable within the context of the proceedings and the work required to be done.

23.15   The 'detailed assessment' process has two important consequences for you. The first is the essential need for you to keep a detailed and accurate record of all work that you do in connection with a case. This should show the details of what work was done, for how long and on what dates. Any expenses claimed by you should also be recorded. The details of the work done should either be shown on the face of your invoice or should be attached as a separate schedule so that the assessing officer has a clear view of what work has been done by you. Appendix 4 provides an example of how a fee note should be produced.

23.16   The second consequence of the 'detailed assessment' procedure and the possibility that your fees may not be allowed as claimed, is that solicitors will wish to protect themselves, their firms or employers from having to pay your fees in full if there is any risk that the court might decide that your fees are unreasonable. This arises because the Legal Services Commission will pay to the solicitor only the amounts authorised by the court. You will find, therefore, that solicitors may seek to obtain your agreement to accepting 'such sum as may be allowed by the court upon detailed assessment'.

23.17   It is a matter for you as to whether you are prepared to undertake the work on that basis. The court will not generally reduce the fees claimed by experts provided that it has full information about the work which has been done, that the hourly rate charged is within the usual band for a person of your level of experience and expertise and the work done was reasonable within the context of the case.

23.18   You are not required to wait until the conclusion of the case to be paid. In a privately funded case you are entitled to be paid following delivery of your invoice. In CLS-funded cases, the scheme allows solicitors to apply for payments on account to cover payment of experts' fees and expenses. A claim for a payment on account will normally be paid by the Legal Services Commission to the solicitor within one month of any claim being submitted. You should therefore be entitled to expect payment within that time unless you have agreed different terms with the solicitor.

23.19   In respect of CLS-funded cases, you may find that many firms will agree to pay only a proportion (typically 75%) of the amount of any fees claimed upon delivery of your invoice before conclusion of the case. This is to protect both you and them from the possibility of the full amount of the fees charged not being allowed upon 'detailed assessment' of their bill of costs. It avoids difficulties which can arise from solicitors having to ask an expert for repayment of part of the fees paid. If the solicitor adopts this practice, it will be made known to you at the time of instruction. It should be a matter for you to decide as to whether you are prepared to work on that basis.

23.20 Many solicitors will now set out their 'Terms of Engagement for Expert Witnesses' in a separate document from the letter of instruction. This will usually be sent with the letter of instruction and will constitute the contractual basis upon which you are being instructed. It is important that you should read and consider the 'Terms of Engagement' since the terms will apply unless you take specific objection to them and agree different terms. An example of such 'Terms of Engagement' is to be found at Appendix 5.

23.21 You may be instructed jointly on behalf of a number of parties to prepare a report. It is important that before accepting such an instruction you are clear as to who is responsible for payment of your fees. Usually the letter of instruction will come from the 'lead' solicitor and should clearly set out who is responsible for payment and how this will be done. In the absence of any express statement or agreement as to how your costs are to be paid and by whom, the responsibility for payments of your fees will fall on the 'lead' solicitor. Good practice would indicate that any order made by the court giving permission for the preparation of an expert's report on the basis of joint instructions should deal with how responsibility for payment of the expert's fees is to be apportioned between the parties. It is worth asking to see the specific terms of any order made. If the order does not deal with the question of how payment is to be dealt with, there is no reason why you should not ask the 'lead' solicitor to take steps to have the order amended to deal with the issue. If that is done, it will avoid the possibility of disputes arising many months later.

23.22 There is an issue about whether or not experts who are given late notice that they are not required to attend to give evidence are entitled to charge 'cancellation' fees. This can also occasionally arise in relation to the late cancellation of meetings which you may have been asked to attend. If you are self-employed and will lose fee income because you are unable to arrange to do other work owing to short notice received to cancel your attendance at court or a meeting for which you have specifically set aside time, you are entitled to be reimbursed provided that this is part of the contract between you and the instructing solicitor. In a CLS-funded case there is no guarantee that such a payment will be allowed on 'detailed assessment'. However, if you wish to be assured of being able to receive payment even though it may be disallowed by the court, you must make this a term or condition of your agreement with the solicitor instructing you who will be duty bound to pay you irrespective of the amount allowed upon 'detailed assessment' or how much he is paid by the Legal Services Commission.

23.23   It is important that you should deliver your invoice as soon as you have completed the work you have done or the case has been concluded. Delay in submitting invoices can create difficulties for you and the solicitor. You should use a simple diary system to record when you have delivered an invoice and when payment of it is expected. If payment has not been made to you within the time scale agreed with the solicitor you should never hesitate to send further reminders. It is often helpful to follow up a written reminder with a telephone call to the solicitor.

23.24   If you have cause for complaint about the way in which you are instructed or are treated by the solicitor instructing you, including the way in which your fees are paid or not paid, you should take this up with the solicitor in writing and make a formal complaint. Every solicitor's practice should have a proper complaints procedure of which you should be given details upon request. If your complaint is not dealt with properly to your satisfaction, the person responsible for dealing with your complaint in the solicitor's practice should provide you with information about other avenues open to you. The Office for the Supervision of Solicitors[3] is responsible for dealing with complaints relating to the professional conduct of solicitors. It will generally entertain a complaint only if the firm's complaints procedure has been invoked and the complaint relates to an issue of 'professional conduct'. It will not generally deal with issues relating to non-payment of fees unless the question of non-payment also includes an issue of 'professional conduct'.

23.25   If your fees are not paid in accordance with the contractual terms agreed between you and the solicitor, it would be open to you to take proceedings for debt recovery in the county court on the basis of breach of contract. This situation should rarely, if ever, arise if the complaints procedures referred to are invoked and properly dealt with. You should always take independent legal advice before issuing proceedings for debt recovery.

Summary

23.26 You should have a written contract or agreement with the instructing solicitor as to the basis upon which you will charge and be paid for work undertaken by you. In cases funded by the CLS you should be aware of what costs limitations apply to the work to be undertaken by you and have that confirmed in writing. You should keep a full record of all work done and ensure that the details are included with your invoice. Keep a diary record of invoices delivered and paid. Do not hesitate to send reminders for payment if payment is not made by the expected or agreed date.

Notes

1   Established under the Access to Justice Act 1999.
2   The Solicitors' Costs and Information and Client Care Code 1999.
3   Office for the Supervision of Solicitors, Victoria Court, 8 Dormer Place, Leamington Spa, CV32 5AE.

Appendix One

Suggested Further Reading

1. *Handbook of Best Practice in Children Act Cases* Children Act Advisory Committee (DOH, June 1997).

2. *The Expert Witness Pack for use in Children Proceedings* produced by the Expert Witness Group (Family Law, 1997).

3. Williams 'Expert Evidence in Cases of Child Abuse' (1993) 68 *Archives of Disease in Childhood* 712.

4. Wall J 'Judicial Attitudes to Expert Evidence in Children's Cases' (1997) 76 *Archives of Disease in Childhood* 485.

5. Hershman and McFarlane 'Pre-trial Liaison between Doctors in Alleged Child Abuse' (1998) *Archives of Disease in Childhood* pp 205–206.

6. Cottrell and Tufnell 'Expert Reports: What Constitutes Good Practice' [1996] Fam Law 159 and Tufnell 'Psychiatric Court Reports in Child Care Cases: What Constitutes "Good Practice"?' (1993) 15 *Association of Child Psychology and Psychiatry Review and Newsletter* pp 219–224.

7. Wall J (ed) *Rooted Sorrows: Psychoanalytic Perspectives on Child Protection, Assessment, Therapy and Treatment* (Family Law, 1997).

8. Walsh *Working in the Family Justice System, A Guide for Professionals* (Family Law, 1998).

9. Black, Harris-Hendriks and Wolkind (eds) *Child Psychiatry and the Law* 3rd edn (Gaskell, 1998).

10. Professor Helen Carty 'Doctor at Law' [1999] Fam Law 391.

11. Plotnikoff and Woolfson *Reporting to Court under the Children Act (A Handbook for Social Services)* (DOH, 1996).

Appendix Two

The Circuits and their Family Division Liaison Judges

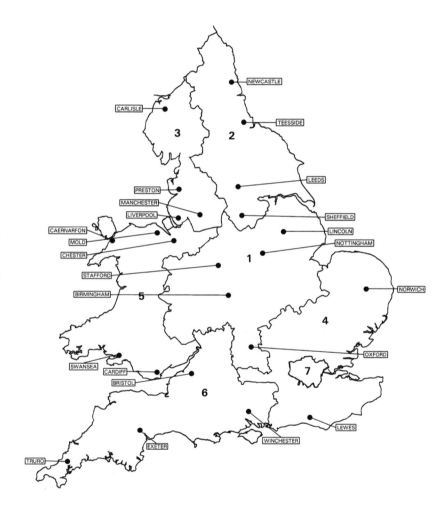

1   Mr Justice Kirkwood (Midland and Oxford Circuit);
2   Mr Justice Singer (North Eastern Circuit);
3   Mr Justice Wall (Northern Circuit);
4   Mr Justice Johnson (South Eastern Circuit);
5   Mr Justice Connell (Wales and Chester Circuit);
6   Mr Justice Holman (Western Circuit);
7   Mr Justice Bodey (Greater London Circuit).

Appendix Three

Extract from the Judgment of Wall J in *Re G (Minors) (Expert Witnesses)* [1994] 2 FLR 291, 298

'In my judgment, the following propositions should govern the grant of leave and consequential directions for expert evidence in children's cases:

1. Generalised orders giving leave for the papers to be shown to "an expert" or "experts" should never be made. In each case the expert or area of expertise should be identified.

2. As part of the process of granting or refusing leave either for the child to be examined or for papers in the case to be shown to an expert, the advocates have a positive duty to place all relevant information before the court and the court has a positive duty to enquire into that information and in particular into the following matters:

    (a) the category of expert evidence which the party in question seeks to adduce;

    (b) the relevance of the expert evidence sought to be adduced to the issues arising for decision in the case;

    (c) whether or not the expert evidence can properly be obtained by the joint instruction of one expert by two or more of the parties;

    (d) whether or not expert evidence in any given category may properly be adduced by only one party (for example by the guardian ad litem) or whether it is necessary for experts in the same discipline to be instructed by more than one party.

3. Where the court exercises its discretion to grant leave for the papers to be shown to a particular expert (whether identified by name or by category of expertise) the court should invariably go on to give directions as to:

    (a) the timescale in which the evidence in question should be produced;

    (b) the disclosure of any report written by an expert both to the parties and to the other experts in the case;

    (c) discussions between experts following future disclosure of reports;

    (d) the filing of further evidence by the experts or the parties stating the areas of agreement and disagreement between the experts.

4. Where it is impractical to give directions under para 3 above at the time leave to disclose the papers is granted, the court should set a date for a further directions appointment at which the directions set out in para 3 can be given.

5. Where it is necessary to consider the estimated length of hearing at a directions appointment the number of expert witnesses and the likely length of their evidence should be carefully considered and the exercise which I have set out in *Re MD and TD (Minors)* undertaken.

6. It is a commonplace of care cases for the local authority to wish at the outset to carry out an assessment. Where this occurs, the court should in my judgment adopt the following approach.

   (a) It should specify the time in which the assessment is to be carried out and direct that evidence of the outcome of the assessment be filed by a given date.

   (b) It should fix a directions appointment for a date immediately after the date fixed for the completion of the assessments to reassess the case and give further directions for a speedy trial.

   (c) Once the local authority assessment is available, immediate thought should be given at the directions appointment following its disclosure to the evidence (expert and otherwise) required to bring the case speedily and fairly to trial. Any directions for expert evidence should identify the areas of expertise for which leave is given and lay down a timetable as per para [3] above.

   (d) Where a date for the final trial can be fixed before the assessment is complete that should be done. More commonly, however, it will only be possible to assess the likely length of a case once the initial assessment is complete and the issues in the case emerge.

It follows that advocates who seek the leave of the court to disclose the papers to an expert must apply their minds at an early stage of the proceedings to the issues in the cases to which medical evidence will be relevant. Applications for leave to instruct experts should thus be made at as early a stage in the proceedings as is possible, commensurate with the state of the evidence. Advocates must come to the directions appointment at which the application is to be decided prepared to satisfy the tribunal as to the need for expert evidence of the specified type sought. Given the pressures of work on expert witnesses, particular experts should be identified and instructed at the earliest possible moment, ...'

Appendix Four

Model Fee Note

Name & address of
instructing solicitors

Case name & court number

To professional fees relating to [describe broad remit of work i.e.
undertaking and reporting on paediatric assessment of ..., or reviewing
medical records and x-rays and providing a report on ... or undertaking
psychiatric/psychological assessment of and a report on ...] to include

Preparation

Date	Perusal & consideration of documents	2.5 hours @ £x	£xxx
Date	Perusal & consideration of further documents preparatory to attending meeting of experts	1.5 hours @ £x	£xxx
Date	Reviewing documents & preparing to attend to give evidence	3.00 hours @ £x	£xxx

Examination/Attendances

Date	Medical/psychiatric/psychological examination of patient/subject	1.5 hours @ £x	£xxx
Date	Further examination of subject	1.00 hour @ £x	£xxx
Date	Attending Meeting of Experts	2.25 hours @ £x	£xxx
Date	Attending conference with counsel/advocate	1.5 hours @ £x	£xxx

Court attendance

Date	Conferring with advocates/other experts	1.25 hours @ £x	£xxx
	Waiting	2.00 hours @ £x	£xxx
	Hearing	2.00 hours @ £x	£xxx

Travelling

Date	Meeting of Medical Experts	2.5 hours @ £x	£xxx
	Conference with counsel	2.00 hours @ £x	£xxx
	Anytown County Court	2.5 hours @ £x	£xxx

Telephone calls/correspondence

Date(s)	Itemise those for which charge to be made	7 @ £x	£xxx

Expenses

Date	Travel [itemise details] x miles @ x pence per mile	£xxx
Date	Parking	£xxx
	Total	**£xxx**

Appendix Five

Expert Witness Terms of Engagement in Legally Aided Children Act Proceedings

[*Name of Firm*] holds a Legal Services Commission Franchise Contract in Family Law. This imposes obligations and requirements which the practice must fulfil in relation to the provision of services to clients who are funded by the Community Legal Service. Experts instructed by [*Name of Firm*] have to be identified as being able to provide a standard and quality of service which enable us to be able to meet our franchise obligations. Experts who fail to meet those standards cannot remain on or be placed on the list of "Approved Experts" which the practice is required to maintain and review on a continuing basis.

Solicitors undertaking Community Legal Service Fund work have a duty to the Legal Services Commission, and their clients, to ensure that costs and fees incurred in the conduct of any case are reasonably necessary. Under the Funding Code, Solicitors are only permitted to pay such fees to expert witnesses for work undertaken by them as are authorised for payment by the Legal Services Commission. Fees payable are either determined by the Legal Services Commission at the conclusion of the proceedings following assessment of the Solicitors bill of costs or by the Court following a detailed assessment of the Solicitors bill of costs in High Court and county court cases.

The Community Legal Service Scheme contains provisions which allow Solicitors to claim payments on account from the Legal Services Commission to enable fees incurred for work done by experts to be discharged before the proceedings are concluded.

Costs in relation to work undertaken by Experts

1. On delivery of instructions, [*Name of Firm*] undertakes to be responsible for payment of the expert's reasonable charges for work undertaken in accordance with those instructions subject only to any limitation as to the amount payable which might be imposed by the Legal Services Commission upon assessment of the costs or by the Court upon detailed assessment of the costs at the conclusion of the proceedings.

2. The expert agrees that the determination made by either the Legal Services Commission or the Court as to the amount of the fees payable shall be final unless otherwise agreed in writing.

3. No payment will be made to an expert unless a fee note or account has been rendered which sets out specific details of the work which has been undertaken and the time spent indicating (if appropriate) charging rates for different levels of activity undertaken.

4. Upon receipt of a fee note, [*Name of Firm*] will seek to obtain a payment on account from the Legal Services Commission to enable a proportion of not more than 75% of the expert's fees to be paid. Normally, payment will be made within two months of the claim for payment on account being submitted.

5. In the event that costs are assessed at a level below any payments made on account the expert will reimburse the difference to this Firm within 14 days of being notified by us of the outcome of the assessment.

General requirements of Expert Witnesses

As the Children Act jurisdiction has developed, the Courts have clarified and laid down their expectations as to how expert witnesses should fulfil their obligations when instructed. Briefly stated, the primary obligations are:

1. Any report commissioned will be completed and filed within the timescale laid down by the Court.

2. Opinions should only be expressed if genuinely held and are based on all the material facts and documentation available and have been properly researched.

3. All information and documentation seen and considered, together with any research material, information or documentation referred to should be detailed in the report prepared by the expert.

4. Any report prepared by the expert will be filed with the Court and disclosed to all parties and other experts instructed in the case.

5. If a number of experts in the same field are instructed, they will be required to hold discussions with the other experts and to set out, in writing, prior to trial areas of agreement and dispute between them and each expert should normally give an opinion upon each set of competing facts.

Solicitor's Obligations

As Franchise holders, [*Name of Firm*] require any expert instructed by them to be able to comply with the above. To facilitate the work to be undertaken by an expert, [*Name of Firm*] will ensure that any instructions delivered will comply with the following:

1. The expert's availability, and willingness, to accept instructions will have been checked with the expert as will the timescale within which a report can be completed.

2. The schedule of the proposed work, and the estimated fees, will have been discussed and agreed subject to any limitations imposed by the Legal Services Commission or the Courts.

3. A detailed letter of instruction will be provided giving a synopsis of the proceedings, identifying issues which are agreed and disputed and identifying the issues on which opinion is sought including any specific questions which may require to be answered by the expert.

4. The instructions will be accompanied by a properly scheduled bundle of documents relevant to the issues which the expert is being asked to address.

5. Any further relevant information, or other experts' reports obtained prior to trial, will be supplied to the expert for consideration and a request made for a further addendum report, if necessary.

6. Efforts will be made to try and ensure that attendance at experts' meetings, or at the Court to give evidence, will be arranged to suit the expert's convenience and, where possible, the expert's availability will be checked before listing the case for trial.

7. If information is subsequently received that an expert's attendance at a trial is not going to be required, then the expert will be informed as soon as conveniently possible.

8. [*Name of Firm*] will endeavour to discharge the expert's fees as soon as possible after receipt of an invoice or account subject to the provisos set out above.

Appendix Six

Courts Hearing Family Cases

1. Cases under the Children Act are heard at every level of court within the Family Justice System. What are called 'public law' cases, where a local authority seeks a care or supervision order must be commenced in the Family Proceedings Court, where they are heard by a bench of lay magistrates or, in some cities, by a stipendiary magistrate either sitting alone or with lay justices. However, the more serious or difficult care cases are usually transferred to the county court, where they are heard by circuit judges known as a 'care' judge (that is judges who have attended a training course organised by the Judicial Studies Board): the most difficult or serious are then transferred up to the High Court, where they are heard by judges of the Family Division, or by senior circuit judges who have been given special dispensation to hear High Court cases or by Queen's Counsel sitting as Deputy High Court Judges.

2. Private law cases, that is disputes usually between parents or other family members over residence or contact may be commenced in any level of court and can then be transferred up or down as the seriousness or difficulty of the case requires.

3. In a public law case, you may thus find yourself writing a report for or giving evidence to lay justices or a stipendiary magistrate in the family proceedings court, or a circuit judge in the county court or, in the High Court, a full time High Court Judge, a specially qualified Circuit Judge or Deputy High Court Judge.

4. Lay justices are unlikely to intervene and ask questions in the way that a professional stipendiary magistrate or county court or High Court Judge will do so. In addition, the clerk in the family proceedings court will be a qualified lawyer, who will not only make a note of the evidence, but will advise the magistrates on any point of law or evidence which arises. You should therefore not be surprised if the justices' clerk plays a proactive role in the proceedings.

Appendix Seven

Relevance of the Civil Procedure Rules 1998

Court proceedings under the Children Act 1989 are governed by Part IV of the Family Proceedings Rules 1991 (FPR) as amended. All other civil proceedings are now governed by the Civil Procedure Rules 1998 (CPR). Part 35 of the CPR deals in detail with experts and expert evidence. It includes, for example, a provision (r 35.14) which allows an expert to 'file a written request for directions to assist him in carrying out his functions as an expert' and enables the expert to seek such directions 'without giving notice to any party'. There is no such provision in the FPR.

At the time of writing, Part 35 of the CPR does not apply in proceedings under the Children Act. However, there is nothing in Part 35 which is in any way inconsistent with the practice and procedure relating to experts and expert evidence which has developed over the years in proceedings relating to children. Indeed, many family lawyers would argue that the CPR bring other civil proceedings into line with practice already well established in the Family Division.

It is, however, likely that steps will be taken to harmonise the two sets of rules, and it may well be that the directly relevant sections of Part 35 will be incorporated into the FPR. If this point troubles you, or you are in any doubt about your rights and duties in relation to either set of rules, you should raise this with the solicitor commissioning your report, who will be able to advise you and keep you up to date.

Index

References are to paragraph and appendix numbers.